THE
DAIRY GOOD
COOKBOOK

THE
DAIRY GOOD
COOKBOOK

Everyday Comfort Food
from America's Dairy Farm Families

EDITED BY LISA KINGSLEY
FOREWORD BY CARLA HALL

Andrews McMeel
Publishing®

Kansas City · Sydney · London

This book is dedicated to the nation's nearly 47,000 dairy farm families who, from sunrise to sundown (and into the evening too) each and every day, care for their cows and the land to ensure we all enjoy nutrient-rich, tasty, versatile, and safe milk. Their commitment demonstrates the values, dedication, and legacy of America's dairy farm families.

CONTENTS

PREFACE *by Alexis Glick*

It's an honor and a privilege to share with you my passion and deep affection for America's dairy farmers and those who bring dairy products from around the world to your table. When asked to contribute to this incredible cookbook, I said yes—before they even finished asking the question!

After all, who better than this community of fine men and women—my friends and mentors—who are rooted in tradition, with recipes that have been passed down from generation to generation to share how dairy products can be used to create satisfying and wonderful dishes.

This cookbook embodies the passion, energy, delicious foods, and the love of the great people who inspired and filled these pages. It makes all the sense in the world that these farmers share their secret (and not so secret) family recipes and a piece of the heart and soul of their farms and history. While most of us have heard of the farm-to-table movement, these amazing people live it every day!

Dairy farmers rise before dawn and work tirelessly to support their farms, their families, and their local communities without pomp or circumstance 365 days a year. I have seen it first-hand time and time again. They work hard, wear their passion on their sleeves, care deeply about their farmland and the animals they care for, and are committed to their communities and our nation's youth.

Dairy farmers and dairy importers are the reason GENYOUth and the Fuel Up to Play 60 program exist today. They represent our greatest asset, giving so much more than dollars to nurture our nation's youth. We developed many of our most valuable health strategies and our

prevention platform for the country's largest in-school health and wellness program, Fuel Up to Play 60 (now in 73,000 schools that impact thirty million kids every day), by learning from the work ethic, health and wellness investment, and DNA of the dairy farmers we call our collaborators and friends. Their commitment to sustainability—the land, animals, natural resources, and future generations—is a practice that we apply to our work each and every day.

I am humbled to present you with this fabulous collection of hearty, wholesome, and downright delicious recipes. In addition to getting time-tested dishes that up until now were shared only among close friends and family, your purchase of this cookbook helps support the GENYOUth Foundation to provide Fuel Up to Play 60 grants to schools and help millions of children get better access to healthful foods.

You're helping students FUEL UP to become healthy, high-achieving adults. Change starts by believing in each other and in our commitment to our local communities and future generations. It will continue, thanks to America's dairy farmers and importers and YOU.

Wishing you wonderful memories with family and friends cooking in the kitchen, eating at your dinner table, exploring our farms, and sharing these dairy farmer recipes from a wealth of treasured family secrets!

Alexis Glick serves as chief executive officer of the GENYOUth Foundation, which is on a mission to inspire and educate youth to improve their nutrition and increase physical activity. GENYOUth was founded through an unprecedented public-private partnership with the National Dairy Council (NDC) and the National Football League (NFL) and their commitment to children's health and wellness. The flagship program, Fuel Up to Play 60, is the largest health and wellness program in schools across the country. GENYOUth is collaborating with students, schools, communities, business partners, and thought leaders to build a platform with the flexibility and energy to make a lasting difference in children's lives.

FOREWORD *by Carla Hall*

According to my maternal grandmother, Freddie Mae (or Granny, as we called her), dairy runs in my family's veins. It was only her father who was a dairy farmer, but every time we had milk, buttermilk, ice milk (as opposed to ice cream), butter, cottage cheese, boiled custard, and all the other things a good Southern grandmother would supply her grandbabies, she would remind my cousins, my sister, and me, "My daddy was a dairy farmer."

She was proud of that fact, so I grew up just as proud. The antique milk can that graced her carport became a symbol of her youth as well as mine. She and my mother would talk about drinking buttermilk as their dinner beverage of choice. I guess my sister and I weren't so lucky.

I came to appreciate good butter and milk long before I attempted to cook my first dish. I don't think I ever had a cold piece of cornbread at my grandmother's house when I was growing up, because she would never make it until we were all on the right side of the door at her house for Sunday supper. There was something magical about watching a big pat of pale yellow, sweet goodness melt into the golden top and crevices of my grandmother's skillet cornbread. The creaminess of the butter was like the cherry on top of an ice cream sundae.

As a chef, I carry many memories of eating at both my grandmothers' homes, and those memories influence my cooking style—Southern with a twist. In my new cookbook, *Carla's Comfort Foods*, I use a traditional smothered chicken recipe with milk gravy to show how you can use the same method and travel the globe right at your stovetop by swapping dairy and other spices. If you want to take your taste buds to Hungary, add sweet paprika instead of thyme, and sour cream instead of milk. If France is more your style, substitute white wine, Dijon mustard, tarragon, and heavy cream. Whether it's milk, sour cream, or heavy cream in your sauce over chicken, at the end of the day I say it's all smothered chicken.

I grew up with dairy being a fabric of my childhood, and later of my professional career—so I know comfort food. And who better to share a number of comfort food recipes that feature dairy than the people who know it best—America's dairy farmers and those who bring dairy from around the world to your dinner table every day.

Carla Hall, cohost of ABC's The Chew, *first made her way into America's heart as a finalist in season five of the award-winning Bravo show,* Top Chef. *Today, Carla continues to bring a passion to cooking, balancing her Southern traditions, classic French training, and holistic approach to food as an entertaining expert and owner and executive chef of Alchemy caterers in Washington, D.C. A native of Nashville, Carla's charm and experience make her a natural teacher. Dedicated to sharing her philosophy of how to "cook with love," Carla has passed on her genuine love and joy for being in the kitchen by teaching at CulinAerie and L'Academie de Cuisine. Carla is a believer that, "if you're not in a good mood, the only thing you should make is a reservation."*

SPECIAL PEOPLE

The real story of the dairy industry is in the people from across the country who care for the cows. They and their love of these marvelous animals give dairy its unique niche in the world of agriculture.

It all started with a cow. Red Larson remembers her like it was yesterday. "I had a paper route and I saved up enough money to buy a Guernsey cow for sixty-five dollars," he recalls. It was an enormous amount, given that it was the middle of the Depression. "We used her for family milk and sold any extra to neighbors. When I got more money, I bought more cows."

Indeed. He and Reda, his wife of sixty-six years, kept adding cows and moving around south Florida as population shifts pushed the farm farther out. Now their family milks 7,500 Holsteins on four different farms, mostly in Okeechobee County in the south-central part of the state.

At ninety, Red comes as close as you can get to being the patriarch of the dairy industry— admired, respected, and honored by generations of dairy farmers and industry organizations across the country. On his ninetieth birthday in March 2014, he was honored by Congress for his outstanding contributions to agriculture.

The U.S. dairy industry is full of astounding facts: nine million dairy cows, nearly 47,000 commercial dairy farms, twenty-three billion gallons of milk a year, ten billion pounds of cheese, and yogurt consumption ticking ever upward at fourteen pounds per person per year.

But the real story of the dairy industry is in the people who tend the cows. They and their love of those marvelous animals make dairy a very special business. If you don't believe it, spend a little time with Red Larson and some of his fellow milk producers. "I've slowed down," Red says of his current farm workload, though one would wonder what he did prior to "slowing down." He says, "I'm in the farm office maybe five or six hours a day, then I try to visit two of our farm operations every day after the office work. That's my favorite thing, talking to the people doing the work. I've been there and done that myself, so I know what it's like. And I want them to know that I have an interest in what they are doing and how hard they work."

Within these pages, you'll also get to know Audrey Donahoe. Put her in front of a crowd and ask her to talk about the dairy business, and you've just flipped the "on" switch. "I want people to know what we do here," she says. "Lots of people have preconceptions about farms and farmers, and they're not good ones. Well, I can answer their questions and tell them exactly how it is. I cherish these opportunities."

Audrey and her husband, Jeff, milk one hundred registered Holstein and Brown Swiss cows near Frankfort, New York. They call it ATRASS Farm, after the names of their six children—Arnold, Tom, Rick, Allison, Sam, and Seth. School tours are her specialty, and because the farm sits prominently on a major road, sometimes complete strangers stop in unannounced just out of curiosity. "I take the time to show them around. I'm completely open, I want them to see it all," Audrey says. "It's because of them that I can do what I do. If I were them, I'd want to know how my food is produced."

Then there are the Hofwegans of Stanfield, Arizona. Don and Ingrid have three to four months of the year when the average daily high temperature is 105 degrees. "We have to work very hard to keep the cows comfortable on those days," Don says.

They do it with a unique system of overhead shades and powerful misters pushing water through giant cooling fans. "We can keep the cows at about eighty-five degrees under the shades," says Don. They're never uncomfortable, and milk production never misses a beat due to heat, he says.

"I like the freedom the farm life gives me," Don says. "I can manage myself and my own business. I get to work with the land and the animals and see the fruits that come from that every day."

Meet Jennifer Holle. She and Andrew, a fourth-generation dairy farmer, met in college. Jennifer had experience with horses but not cows. "How was I going to find a niche on a dairy farm?" she wondered. She found a way, however. "I took on the baby calves," she says. "They're a little bit similar to caring for horses."

She and Andrew have 600 Holsteins in partnership with his parents, Kenton and Bobby Jo, at a farm they call Northern Lights Dairy located in Mandan, North Dakota. They also have a growing family of four children. "We love what we do," says Jennifer. "We're doing it all with our family—our kids and my husband's parents. It's not really a job, it's who we are."

That's the heart of the American dairy industry—quality products for your family, originating with the interaction of dairy cows and farm families simply being "who we are." As you enjoy the recipes and stories in *The Dairy Good Cookbook,* remember: It's a very special group.

The Dairy Good Cookbook is unlike any other cookbook. The book is organized around a dairy farmer's day, beginning with a "Sunrise Breakfast" and ending with "After-Dinner Dessert," along with other special days that include holidays and get-togethers. Along with profiles of large and small dairy farms, each chapter also highlights one of six different types of dairy cows. More than one hundred recipes showcase dairy in many forms, from cheese to yogurt, milk, and butter. Nothing soothes the soul like a warm bite of Salsa Mac with Colby Jack (page 164), Apple-Cheddar Pizza (page 74), Apricot-Dijon Pork Chops (page 140), or a taste of Triple-Layer Chocolate Cake with Vanilla Buttercream (page 202).

In addition to recipes, this book offers cooking notes about how to optimize the taste and performance of dairy, including sour cream, buttermilk, and crème fraîche. Each recipe highlights interesting tidbits, such as its possible origin or the contributor's story of how the dish was originally prepared and served. Tips on freezing, storing, and making ahead are featured as well. Classic favorites, such as macaroni and cheese and dessert crepes, are included, with new twists and flavor combinations that add color and taste to mealtimes.

The Dairy Good Cookbook is a celebration of all things dairy: an inside look at the world of the dairy farm family, the cows that make it all possible, and the flavorful and fun-to-cook family meals that America loves to eat.

DAIRY COOKING NOTES

Milk and all the wonderful products made from it are an integral part of cooking and baking. Knowing the qualities of dairy ingredients, which is the best type for your particular recipe—and how to properly use it—will make your casseroles, cookies, and cakes turn out perfectly every time.

BUTTER Cream is churned until it reaches a semisolid state to make this sunny yellow stuff. According to law, butter must be at least eighty percent milkfat. The U.S. Department of Agriculture grades and scores butter on a variety of qualities, including flavor, body, texture, color, and salt. Butter is sometimes colored with annatto, a common coloring agent that is derived from the seeds of the achiote tree, to boost its naturally pale yellow hue. Butter is sold both salted and unsalted. In general, unsalted butter is best for baking and salted butter is best for all other uses. Butter most commonly comes in 1-pound blocks or packages of four quarter-pound sticks. Each stick equals ½ cup butter.

BUTTERMILK In the days when most people made their own butter, buttermilk was the liquid left over after the butter was churned. Today, it is made by adding beneficial bacteria to fat-free or low-fat milk, which thickens it and gives it a distinctive tanginess. Buttermilk makes pancakes and baked goods especially light and tender, but it can affect the rise. If you'd like to substitute buttermilk for regular milk in any leavened recipe, adjust the baking soda/baking powder ratio. In general, substitute some or all of any baking powder for baking soda. The rule is for each cup of buttermilk used in place of regular milk, reduce the baking powder by 2 teaspoons and replace it with ½ teaspoon baking soda.

CHEESE Given the breadth and variety of this wonderful food, the ingredients are incredibly simple: milk, salt, rennet (or other enzymes), and time. The conditions under which a cheese is aged and how long it is aged determine its flavor, texture, and meltability. Fresh cheeses such as feta, queso fresco, and fresh mozzarella are not aged at all or not aged very long. Soft or semisoft cheeses such as Havarti and Muenster are aged two to three months. Medium-hard cheeses such as Gouda are aged a little longer, and semihard or hard cheeses such as Cheddar and Colby can be aged for months or even years. Cheeses along the soft to semihard spectrum have the best meltability. The hardest cheeses—the most popular is Parmesan—also are called "grating cheeses" because they hold their shape well when grated. They are the driest cheeses and have the least meltability.

COTTAGE CHEESE This mild, moist fresh cheese is made from whole, part-skimmed, or skimmed cow's milk. It comes in three forms—small curd, medium curd, and large curd—and is usually enjoyed as a side dish or snack. Creamed cottage cheese has four to eight percent cream added to it. Other types contain zero to two percent fat.

CREAM When unhomogenized milk stands, it naturally separates into two layers—cream on top and nearly fat-free milk on the bottom. The cream you buy at the supermarket has been pasteurized and commercially separated, of course, but it is the same principle at work. There are actually several types of cream, depending on how much milkfat it contains. Light cream usually contains twenty percent milkfat and cannot be whipped. Light whipping cream—the type most commonly found in the supermarket and most commonly used in cooking—contains thirty to thirty-six percent fat. Heavy cream—between thirty-six and forty percent milkfat—is usually only available at specialty markets. Fun fact: Whipping cream doubles in volume when whipped.

CREAM CHEESE William Lawrence, a Chester, New York, dairyman, developed this mildly tangy, spreadable cheese in 1872. It is a soft, unripened cheese made from cow's milk and contains, by law, a minimum of thirty percent milkfat. There are lower-fat and fat-free varieties available as well. Reduced-fat cream cheese (or Neufchâtel) can be substituted in most recipes with minimal impact on texture and flavor.

CRÈME FRAÎCHE This thickened cream of French origin has a tangy flavor and velvety rich texture that ranges from the consistency of sour cream to nearly solid. It can be found in specialty markets and in some supermarkets. It is often added to sauces because it can be boiled without curdling. It's also wonderful spooned over fresh berries or warm fruit desserts.

HALF-AND-HALF Equal parts milk and cream, this is the standard addition to coffee for those who don't take it black. If you are trying to reduce the fat and calories in some recipes that call for cream—such as soups or pastas—half-and-half makes a good substitute.

MILK This is where it all starts. Whether you prefer whole milk (three and one-half to four percent milkfat), reduced-fat milk (two percent milkfat) low-fat milk (one percent milkfat) or fat-free milk (zero percent milkfat), milk is a nutritional boon. It contains calcium, potassium, phosphorus, protein, riboflavin, niacin, and vitamins A, D, and B12. Milk produced and sold commercially in the United States is safe and of the highest quality.

It is pasteurized to destroy microorganisms that can cause disease and homogenized to ensure a uniformly smooth product. All of the recipes in this book were tested with whole milk, so when a recipe calls for "milk," whole milk is assumed for optimum richness and flavor. If you prefer to use the variety of milk options available, you can substitute a lower-fat milk for whole milk in some cases—such as in a cake or quick bread—without affecting the flavor and texture of the finished product very much. However, in a soup or pasta dish, it's best to use whole milk.

RICOTTA Perhaps the greatest misnomer about ricotta is that it's cheese. It is a dairy product—thought to be a by-product of Italy's cheesemaking industry. It contains neither starter nor rennet. Rather, it is made by removing the solids that form when whey is reheated. In fact, "ricotta" means "recooked" in Italian. The result is a creamy, mild, subtly sweet, slightly grainy "cheese." American ricottas are made with a combination of whey and whole or skim milk. Ricotta comes in whole-milk, part-skim, and nonfat varieties. While nonfat ricotta saves on fat grams and calories, whole-milk or part-skim ricotta imparts richer flavor and texture.

SOUR CREAM What would a baked potato be without butter and sour cream? To make sour cream, a lactic acid culture is added to cream to thicken it and impart a delicious tanginess. Regular sour cream contains between eighteen and twenty percent milkfat. Light sour cream—made from half-and-half—has about forty percent less fat than regular sour cream. Nonfat sour cream contains zero percent milkfat. While nonfat sour cream is fine as a topping, it's best to cook with regular or light sour cream.

YOGURT The refreshingly tart taste of yogurt is the result of healthful bacteria being introduced into milk. It is made from whole, reduced-fat, and skim milk, and is sold plain or flavored. While regular yogurt is strained twice, Greek yogurt is strained three times. The result is thicker and more concentrated. Use interchangeably in most recipes, depending on the texture you prefer—loose and light or thick and creamy.

SUNRISE
breakfast

EGGS · PANCAKES · WAFFLES · BREAKFAST BREADS
PASTRIES · COFFEE CAKES · SMOOTHIES · GRITS

RECIPES

BLUEBERRY CRUMBLE BAR

A creamy topping of vanilla yogurt and blueberries crowns a buttery oat crust in this breakfast treat. It's served chilled, so it can be made the night before you serve it. If you're chilling it for longer than two hours, cover with plastic wrap.

CRUST

- 1 cup all-purpose flour
- 1 cup quick-cooking rolled oats
- ⅔ cup packed light brown sugar
- ¼ teaspoon baking soda
- ½ cup (1 stick) unsalted butter

FILLING

- 1 large egg
- 2 tablespoons cornstarch
- 4 cups vanilla Greek yogurt
- ½ cup granulated sugar
- 2 cups blueberries, fresh or frozen
- 1 tablespoon flour (optional)

1. Preheat the oven to 350°F. For the crust, combine the flour, oats, brown sugar, and baking soda in a medium mixing bowl. Using a pastry blender, cut in the butter until the mixture resembles coarse crumbs. Press into the bottom of an ungreased 9-by-9-inch baking pan; set aside.

2. For the filling, whisk the egg and cornstarch in a large mixing bowl. Add the yogurt and granulated sugar; stir until blended. If using frozen blueberries, toss them with 1 tablespoon flour. Fold the berries into the yogurt mixture. Pour the filling evenly over the crust.

3. Bake for 1 hour or until a toothpick inserted in the center comes out clean. Cool on a wire rack for 30 minutes. Chill in the refrigerator for at least 2 hours before serving. Cut into 9 (3-inch) squares to serve.

APPLE-PECAN COFFEE CAKE

This cinnamon-and-ginger-spiced coffee cake can be made with a variety of apples. Tart Granny Smiths hold their shape well when baked or cooked. A sweeter apple, such as Honeycrisp, Fuji, or Gala works beautifully too—or use a mix.

STREUSEL

- ¾ cup firmly packed dark brown sugar
- 4 tablespoons unsalted butter, melted
- ⅓ cup all-purpose flour
- ⅓ cup pecan pieces, toasted

CAKE

- Softened butter, for the baking pan
- 3 cups all-purpose flour
- ½ teaspoon ground ginger
- ½ teaspoon ground cinnamon
- 1 tablespoon baking powder
- ½ teaspoon salt
- ½ cup (1 stick) unsalted butter, softened
- 1⅓ cups granulated sugar
- 2 large eggs
- 1 cup milk
- ½ teaspoon vanilla extract
- 3 apples, peeled, cored, and cut into ½-inch pieces

1. For the streusel, combine the brown sugar, butter, flour, and pecans in a small bowl; set aside.

2. Preheat the oven to 350°F. For the cake, butter the bottom and sides of a 9-by-13-inch baking pan. Whisk the flour, ginger, cinnamon, baking powder, and salt in a medium mixing bowl.

3. Combine the butter and sugar in a large mixing bowl. Beat with an electric mixer on medium-high speed until light and fluffy, scraping down the sides of the bowl as necessary. Add the eggs, one at a time, beating well after each addition.

4. Stir together the milk and vanilla in a small bowl. Alternately add the milk mixture and the flour mixture to the butter mixture in three additions, mixing well after each addition. Stir in the apples.

5. Spread half the batter in the prepared pan. Sprinkle half the streusel over the batter. Spread the remaining batter over the streusel. Sprinkle the remaining streusel over the top.

6. Bake for 30 minutes or until a cake tester or skewer inserted in the middle comes out clean. Cool on a wire rack for 30 minutes before cutting. To store, cool the cake completely. Cover with aluminum foil and store at room temperature up to 2 days.

FRESH BERRY–STUFFED FRENCH TOAST WITH VANILLA YOGURT SAUCE

Each bite of the custardy French toast is complemented by juicy, sweet-tart berries. A drizzle of sauce made with yogurt, berries, and sweetened condensed milk is a tasty alternative to syrup.

2 cups mixed fresh berries, such as blueberries, sliced strawberries, raspberries, or blackberries

2 tablespoons powdered sugar

1/3 cup sweetened condensed milk

1 (6-ounce) container vanilla yogurt

1 (10-ounce) loaf French bread

1 large egg

1 large egg white

1/3 cup milk

1 teaspoon granulated sugar

1 teaspoon vanilla extract

1/4 teaspoon ground cinnamon

2 tablespoons unsalted butter

Mixed fresh berries, for serving

1. Combine the 2 cups berries and the powdered sugar in a medium bowl and stir gently to combine. For the sauce, combine 1/2 cup of the sweetened berries, the sweetened condensed milk, and the yogurt in a blender. Blend until smooth; set aside.

2. Preheat the oven to 225°F. Cut the bread into eight 1½-inch slices. Cut into each piece almost all the way through to create a pocket. Stuff each pocket with 3 tablespoons of the remaining sweetened berries then press lightly to close; set aside.

3. Whisk the egg, egg white, milk, granulated sugar, vanilla, and cinnamon in a medium bowl. Melt 1 tablespoon of the butter in a large skillet over medium heat. Dip the stuffed bread slices in the egg mixture to coat. Cook in the skillet until lightly browned on both sides, about 2 minutes, turning once. Add more butter to the pan as needed. Place the cooked bread slices on a large platter and keep warm in the oven while you cook the remaining slices.

4. Place two stuffed slices on each of four serving plates. Top with mixed berries and serve with the yogurt-berry sauce and fresh berries.

PREP: 15 minutes COOK: 2 minutes MAKES: 2 servings

WAFFLE PANINI WITH MAPLE BUTTER, BACON, AND CHEDDAR

This simple breakfast sandwich hits a whole host of tastes—sweet syrup, salty and smoky bacon, and tangy white Cheddar. Pure maple syrup makes a big difference in the intensity of the flavor in the maple butter. Use leftover maple butter on toast, pancakes, or warm biscuits.

½ cup (1 stick) butter, softened
3 tablespoons pure maple syrup
4 frozen waffles, thawed
4 slices white Cheddar cheese
1 apple or pear
4 slices peppered bacon, cooked

1. For the maple butter, combine the butter and maple syrup in a medium mixing bowl and beat with an electric mixer until smooth and fluffy. Transfer to a 6-ounce ramekin. If not using immediately, cover and chill until ready to use. (Any leftover butter can be stored, covered, in the refrigerator for up to 2 weeks; allow to come to room temperature before using.)

2. Spread one side of each waffle with some of the maple butter. Top the buttered side of two of the waffles with one slice of cheese each. If desired, peel the apple or pear. Slice the apple or pear into thin slices. Divide the fruit slices between the two waffles on top of the cheese. Top each

with two slices of cooked bacon. Top with another slice of cheese. Place a second waffle, buttered side down, on each stacked waffle.

3. Melt about 1 tablespoon of the maple butter in a skillet over medium heat. Place the panini in the pan. Weight with a heavy skillet. Cook for 1 to 2 minutes or until the waffles are toasted. Turn panini over, weight, and cook for 1 to 2 minutes more or until the waffles are toasted and the cheese is melted. Serve immediately.

Pancake Stratas, page 30

PANCAKE STRATAS

When you can't decide what you want for breakfast, this hearty stack has it all—pancakes, cheesy scrambled eggs, sausage, and blueberry compote (see page 28). A drizzle of maple syrup and pat of butter right before serving make it even better!

½ cup granulated sugar

4 cups fresh blueberries, divided

2 teaspoons cornstarch

4 cups ready-made pancake batter

8 large eggs

½ cup milk

1 teaspoon salt

½ teaspoon freshly ground black pepper

2 cups shredded sharp Cheddar cheese

12 ounces chicken-apple sausage links or link breakfast sausage of choice, sliced ¼ inch thick

2 teaspoons vegetable oil

Maple syrup (optional)

6 pats butter (optional)

1. For the blueberry compote, combine ½ cup water, the sugar, and 2 cups of the blueberries in a small saucepan over medium heat. Bring to a boil. Turn the heat down to low and simmer, stirring occasionally, until the mixture thickens slightly and the berries begin to break down, 6 to 8 minutes. Stir together the cornstarch and 2 teaspoons cold water. Stir into the blueberry mixture. Cook and stir until the sauce thickens enough to coat the back of a spoon, 3 to 4 minutes; set aside.

2. Using the pancake batter, cook 12 pancakes according to the package instructions; cover lightly to keep warm.

3. Whisk the eggs, milk, salt, and pepper in a large bowl. Stir in the shredded cheese. In a large nonstick skillet, cook the sausage slices in the oil over medium heat for 3 to 5 minutes or until browned. Add the egg mixture and cook, stirring often, until the eggs are firm but still creamy, 3 to 5 minutes.

4. To assemble the stratas, place one pancake on a plate. Top with about ¾ cup of the scrambled egg mixture. Place a second pancake on top. Top with some of the blueberry compote, some of the remaining fresh blueberries, and, if desired, maple syrup and a pat of butter. Repeat to make a total of six stratas.

MOTHER'S DAY BRUNCH
Frosty Pineapple-Orange Smoothies (page 35)
Pancake Stratas
Apple-Pecan Coffeecake (page 23)
Coffee

CINNAMON SWIRL YOGURT START-UPS

This extra-special take on French toast—made with cinnamon swirl bread and topped with flavored yogurt and fresh fruit—takes the same time to make as plain French toast. If you'd like, use Greek yogurt in place of regular yogurt. Greek yogurt gives the topping tangy taste, with slightly thicker texture.

FRENCH TOAST

2   large eggs

½   cup milk

¼   teaspoon ground cinnamon
     Nonstick cooking spray

4   pieces cinnamon swirl bread

TOPPING

1   cup plain yogurt

¼   cup orange juice

2   tablespoons maple syrup

1   cup chopped fresh fruit (any combination)

1. For the French toast, beat together the eggs, milk, and cinnamon in a medium bowl. Lightly coat a nonstick skillet with nonstick cooking spray and preheat over medium heat. Dip each piece of bread into the egg mixture to coat thoroughly. Place in the skillet and cook for about 2 minutes on each side.

2. For the topping, combine the yogurt, orange juice, and maple syrup in a small bowl.

3. For each serving, cut the warm French toast on the diagonal. Arrange on a plate. Top with the fruit and drizzle with the yogurt topping.

HOLSTEIN

THE GENTLE GIANTS These (most often) black-and-white cows weigh 1,500 pounds or more when mature, and they dominate the dairy industry today. Of the nearly nine million dairy cows in the United States, more than ninety percent are Holsteins.

STRENGTHS Dairy farmers opt to raise and milk Holsteins based on their ability to produce far more milk than other breeds. The average Holstein produces about 2,800 gallons per year, according to the National Dairy Herd Improvement Association. That's twenty-five percent more than the average of any other breed.

ORIGIN Holsteins came to the United States in 1852 from the Netherlands.

"WOW" COW The world record for milk production in one year was set by a Holstein, Ever-Green-View My 1326-ET. She produced 8,400 gallons of milk! That's an average of 23 gallons each day. She's owned by Thomas Kestell of Ever-Green-View Farm near Waldo, Wisconsin.

"She's ten years old now," Thomas says, "and weighs about 1,800 pounds. She's very efficient at converting feed and water into milk." For that reason, her offspring are in demand all over the world. Many of her daughters are in the milking herd at Ever-Green-View Farm, and more are on the way, Thomas says. "These Holstein cows are world-famous," adds Chris Kestell, Tom's son. "We like them because they're so productive. They're being used to upgrade dairy genetics in many countries."

APPLE-YOGURT SMOOTHIES

Adding an apple to a smoothie gives it body and a shot of fiber. To maximize the amount of fiber in these smoothies, don't peel the apple.

2 cups vanilla yogurt

1 Granny Smith apple, cored, peeled, and diced

½ cup orange juice

½ cup ice

2 tablespoons honey

Sliced almonds, mint leaves, dash of cinnamon, for garnish

1. Blend the yogurt, apple, orange juice, ice, and honey in a blender until smooth.

2. Divide between two glasses. Garnish with sliced almonds, mint leaves, and cinnamon.

FROSTY PINEAPPLE-ORANGE SMOOTHIES

Egg white powder adds protein to this smoothie, but it also helps whip and froth the texture. Look for powdered egg whites (sometimes called meringue powder) in the baking aisle of a supermarket.

1½ cups chilled orange juice
½ cup pineapple chunks, drained
1¼ cups vanilla yogurt
½ cup ice
1 teaspoon powdered egg whites

1. Combine the orange juice, pineapple, yogurt, and ice in a blender. Blend on high speed for 2 minutes. Add the egg white powder and blend until frothy.

2. Divide between two glasses and serve immediately.

The scale of the equipment and the storage capacities have grown tremendously on America's dairy farms. Yet basic functions endure: growing and storing feed, nurturing and milking cows.

MANGO-YOGURT SMOOTHIE

This fruity smoothie is light and refreshing—a perfect grab-and-go breakfast for a busy morning when it's warm outside and you want something cool and quick. It's very similar to a popular chilled Indian drink called mango *lassi*, which can be also be made with buttermilk or extra-rich milk.

1 (6-ounce) container plain yogurt

1 cup frozen mango chunks

1 teaspoon honey

Fresh mint leaves, for garnish (optional)

1. Blend the yogurt, mango chunks, and honey in a blender until smooth.

2. Pour into a tall glass and garnish with mint leaves, if desired. Serve immediately.

EGGS IN A POCKET

A hearty breakfast of cheesy scrambled eggs and toast becomes a go-anywhere, fork-free meal with the eggs neatly tucked into a toasted pita bread half. Kick up the flavor with bacon, zesty jalapeño or Monterey Jack cheese or add chopped mushrooms, onions, or green peppers to the eggs before scrambling.

½ whole wheat or regular pita bread
2 teaspoons butter
2 large eggs, beaten
1 tablespoon milk
Salt
Freshly ground black pepper
¼ cup shredded Cheddar cheese

1. Toast the pita in a nonstick skillet over medium heat, turning once. Remove the pita from the skillet and set aside.

2. Melt the butter in the same nonstick skillet over medium heat. Beat the eggs, milk, salt, black pepper to taste, and cheese in a small bowl. Cook the eggs in the skillet until set and the cheese is melted. Fill the pita pocket with the eggs. Serve immediately.

A couple of dedicated people and a herd of gentle Jersey cows can serve as a perfect recipe for a dairy farm. Dairy work is seldom a one-person operation as farmers rely on a team of expert professionals to help ensure care and quality.

"Our cows are out grazing in a pasture or eating hay forages grown on our farm. We think it's the best system for them." —Laura Chase, Maine dairy farmer

VAUGHN & LAURA CHASE MAPLETON, MAINE

Just a half hour from Maine's Canadian border, Vaughn and Laura Chase and their family milk cows in a place where the phrase "bone-chilling cold" isn't strong enough. "We sometimes have the distinction of being singled out as the coldest spot in the continental United States," says Laura of their frequent thirty-degrees-below-zero temperatures.

Surprisingly, the Chases' red-and-white Holsteins don't let the cold bother them much. "Except for the very coldest or snowiest days, they go outside," says Laura. The herd totals one hundred head of the distinctive red-and-whites (most Holsteins are black-and-white).

"Vaughn has always liked the red cows," says Laura. "They're really gentle. We had some fourth-graders here and they walked right up and petted some of the cows in the pasture. It was one of those perfect springlike days that could make you forget it's January."

Dairy farmers have many options in running their farm businesses, including producing organic milk. The Chases opted for organic milk certification a few years ago because their production practices were nearly organic anyway.

"Our cows are out grazing in a pasture or eating hay forages grown on our farm," Laura says. "We think it's the best system for them."

Lewis, the oldest Chase child, works full time on the farm with his parents. Daughter April helps when she's home from college. Brooke and Cole are still at home and help too. "We love this life because we get to spend a lot of time outdoors with our family," says Laura. "It doesn't get any better than that."

See Laura's recipe for Pearline's Salmon Stew on page 53.

POWER-UP MUFFIN CUPS

Everybody seems to love strata—that savory combination of bread, eggs, milk, and cheese that is most often reserved for special-occasion brunches. These high-protein mini stratas are made in muffin cups and only have to soak for ten minutes (instead of overnight) for a satisfying hot breakfast any day of the week.

	Nonstick cooking spray
8	large eggs
1¼	cups plain 2% Greek yogurt
1	teaspoon onion powder
1	teaspoon garlic powder
½	teaspoon salt
¼	teaspoon freshly ground black pepper
1¼	cups shredded mozzarella cheese, divided
1¼	cups shredded Cheddar cheese
1½	cups frozen chopped broccoli, thawed
1½	cups cubed whole-grain bread

1. Preheat the oven to 375°F. Coat a standard 12-cup nonstick muffin tin with nonstick cooking spray.

2. Beat the eggs and yogurt until thoroughly combined in a large bowl. Whisk in the onion powder, garlic powder, salt, and pepper. Stir in ¾ cup of the mozzarella cheese, all of the Cheddar cheese, the broccoli, and the bread; mix thoroughly.

3. Let stand for 10 minutes. Stir thoroughly, then divide the mixture evenly among prepared muffin cups. (The cups will be about two-thirds full.) Top evenly with the remaining ½ cup shredded mozzarella cheese.

4. Bake for 20 to 25 minutes or until the tops are golden brown. Let stand for 5 minutes before serving.

Dairy cows and the people who care for them are bonded by much more than milk. It's often a lifelong relationship that can be both tender and personal.

PEPPER AND EGG BRUNCH BAKE

Red and green peppers make this easy egg bake from the Holter family of Pomeroy, Ohio, perfect for a holiday brunch. The Holters operate a multigenerational dairy farm that began in 1946 with fifteen cows and ninety acres and has grown to 200 cows and 525 acres. Kelsey Holter—granddaughter of farm founder Roy Holter—says that dairy farming "becomes your life. It's what you believe in and it's your passion."

6 large eggs, beaten

3 cups milk

2 cups shredded Cheddar, Colby, or Monterey Jack cheese (8-ounce package)

1 teaspoon ground mustard

¼ teaspoon salt

¼ teaspoon freshly ground black pepper

6 cups cubed country-style sourdough or whole-wheat bread

1 13-ounce package turkey kielbasa, cut into ¼-inch pieces

1½ cups chopped yellow onions (2 small)

1 cup chopped green bell pepper (1 medium)

1 cup chopped red bell pepper (1 medium)

¼ cup chopped fresh basil

Softened butter, for the baking dish

1. Whisk the eggs, milk, cheese, mustard, salt, and black pepper in a large bowl. Add the bread, kielbasa, onions, and bell peppers. Stir well until the egg mixture is completely absorbed. Cover the bowl and refrigerate for at least 12 hours.

2. Preheat the oven to 350°F. Stir the basil into the egg mixture. Butter a 9 by 13-inch baking dish. Pour the egg mixture into the prepared dish and bake for 1 hour or until the eggs are set. Let stand for 5 to 10 minutes before serving.

SUMMER VEGETABLE FRITTATA

A well-seasoned cast-iron skillet is ideal for making this cheesy, veggie-packed frittata. Cast iron distributes heat evenly and goes from stovetop to oven—and to the table for serving.

8 large eggs

½ cup milk

1 teaspoon salt

1 teaspoon freshly ground black pepper

1 teaspoon fresh thyme

1 teaspoon finely chopped fresh sage

1 cup crumbled feta cheese

1 tablespoon vegetable oil

1 (12-ounce) bunch thin asparagus, trimmed and cut on a diagonal into 1-inch pieces (about 2½ cups)

½ small zucchini or summer squash, trimmed, halved, and sliced into half-moon shapes

2 Roma tomatoes, chopped

1 cup shredded mozzarella cheese

Fresh thyme leaves (optional)

1. Preheat the oven to 400°F. Whisk the eggs, milk, salt, pepper, and herbs in a large bowl. Stir in the feta cheese; set aside.

2. Heat the oil over medium-high heat in a 12-inch oven-safe skillet. When the oil is hot, add the asparagus and cook, stirring occasionally, for 5 minutes or until lightly browned. Add the zucchini and tomatoes and cook for 2 minutes more.

3. Pour the egg mixture over the vegetables, pulling the eggs away from the sides of the pan with a spatula so they flow to the bottom of the pan. Cook for 4 to 5 minutes.

4. When the eggs begin to set, sprinkle the shredded mozzarella over the top. Transfer the skillet to the oven. Bake for 8 to 10 minutes or until the top is golden. Cut into 6 wedges. Sprinkle with fresh thyme leaves, if desired. Serve immediately.

TRIPLE CHEESE–VEGGIE ROLLS

These savory rolls are a nice change of pace from sweet rolls. Scrambled eggs, cheese, and vegetables are rolled up in a pizza crust for a warm, satisfying, portable breakfast.

Nonstick cooking spray

¾ **cup shredded Cheddar cheese**

1 **cup shredded mozzarella cheese**

¾ **cup shredded Colby Jack cheese**

6 **large eggs**

½ **teaspoon salt**

¼ **teaspoon freshly ground black pepper**

1 **(13.8-ounce) tube refrigerated pizza dough**

Flour, as needed

¾ **cup chopped red, green, yellow, or orange bell pepper**

2 **green onions, sliced**

⅓ **cup sliced black olives**

1. Preheat the oven to 350°F. Spray a standard 12-cup muffin tin with nonstick cooking spray; set aside.

2. Combine the cheeses in a large bowl; set aside. Whisk the eggs with the salt and black pepper in a medium bowl. Spray a medium nonstick skillet with nonstick cooking spray. Pour the eggs into the skillet and cook over medium-low heat, stirring frequently, until firm but still creamy, 3 to 5 minutes.

3. Roll out the dough on a floured surface to a 12-by-8-inch rectangle, about ⅛ inch thick. Scatter the cheeses evenly over the surface of the dough, leaving a ½-inch border around all edges. Spread the scrambled eggs evenly on top of the cheese. Scatter the bell pepper, green onions, and black olives over the eggs.

4. Roll up the dough very tight from one long side. Brush water along the edge of the dough and pinch tightly to seal. Using a sharp serrated knife, cut the roll into 12 pieces, about 1 inch wide. Place the pieces, cut side up, in the prepared muffin cups.

5. Bake for 15 to 18 minutes, or until the dough is golden brown. Cool the rolls in the pan on a wire rack for 5 minutes. Remove from the pan and cool on a rack for 5 minutes more before serving.

SPICY SAUSAGE GRITS 'N' CHEESE

Served alone or as a side to a plateful of eggs, these creamy, cheesy grits will wake up your taste buds with great spicy flavor. They're perfect with a cup of strong coffee.

1	(7-ounce) package chorizo
4	cups milk
1	cup quick-cooking grits
¼	teaspoon salt
¼	teaspoon freshly ground black pepper
½	cup shredded mozzarella cheese
½	cup shredded Monterey Jack cheese
½	cup shredded Cheddar cheese, plus more for serving
⅓	cup sliced green onions

1. Cook the chorizo in a medium skillet over medium heat until browned and cooked through, about 8 minutes. Transfer to a paper towel–lined plate to drain; set aside.

2. Bring the milk to a simmer in a large saucepan over medium heat. Whisk the grits, salt, and pepper into the milk and cook, stirring rapidly, for 4 minutes or until the grits thicken. Stir in the cooked chorizo and the cheeses and cook until the cheeses are completely melted and incorporated.

3. Divide the grits among four serving bowls. Sprinkle each serving with green onions and, if desired, additional shredded Cheddar. Serve immediately.

MIDDAY
lunch

SOUPS AND STEWS · SANDWICHES · SALADS
PIZZAS · BURGERS · TACOS · ENCHILADAS · BURRITOS

RECIPES

PEARLINE'S SALMON STEW

Pearline was the mother-in-law of Laura Chase (of Chase's Organic Dairy Farm in Mapleton, Maine—see page 39), who offers this recipe in her honor. Beginning in 1935, Pearline managed an entire dairy farm and still managed to cook three meals a day for four children. Pearline used canned salmon because she lived far from the coast—but you could certainly add about 1½ cups cooked salmon, cut into chunks, if you'd like. The stew is a filling, warming meal on a cold day—and because the ingredients are pantry staples, it can be stirred together on a moment's notice.

4 tablespoons butter

1 large sweet onion, chopped

5 medium russet potatoes, peeled and cubed

2 (14.5-ounce) cans salmon, drained, liquid reserved

6 cups milk

½ teaspoon salt

½ teaspoon freshly ground black pepper

Fresh snipped chives

Oyster crackers or crushed saltines (optional)

1. Melt the butter in a stockpot or Dutch oven over medium heat. Add the onion and cook until softened, 4 to 5 minutes.

2. Add the potatoes and just enough water to cover, about 3 cups. Bring to a boil. Lower the heat and cook, covered, until the potatoes are tender, 10 to 15 minutes. While the potatoes are cooking, transfer the salmon to a plate and remove any skin or bones. Rinse the salmon and, if necessary, break it into large chunks.

3. When the potatoes are cooked, add the salmon, the reserved liquid from the salmon, the milk, and the salt and pepper. Heat on low, stirring occasionally, until the soup is heated through.

4. Ladle into eight bowls. Top each serving with fresh chives and, if desired, oyster crackers or crushed saltines.

CARAWAY CHEESE SOUP

Dairy farmers John and Kim Koepke of Oconomowoc, Wisconsin, make a version of this soup with their own LaBelle cheese with fenugreek, an aromatic seed popular in Indian cooking. Fenugreek has a sweet, nutty, maple-like flavor that perfectly complements the rich, creamy flavor of the cheese. In fact, the Koepkes' recipe includes a bit of pure maple syrup. You can also try this satisfying soup made with Swiss cheese studded with caraway seeds.

3 tablespoons butter

1 cup chopped yellow onion

¼ cup all-purpose flour

3½ cups chicken broth

¼ cup dry white wine

1 bay leaf

½ cup heavy cream

12 ounces Swiss and caraway cheese, shredded

1 teaspoon Worcestershire sauce

½ teaspoon freshly ground black pepper

Toasted seasoned croutons

Cracked black pepper (optional)

1. Melt the butter in a large heavy-bottom soup pot over medium heat. Add the onion. Cook, stirring occasionally, for 5 to 8 minutes, or until the onion begins to soften. Sprinkle the flour over the onion and cook, stirring constantly, for 1 to 2 minutes.

2. Gradually add the chicken broth and wine, whisking constantly. Bring to a boil, whisking frequently. Decrease the heat to low and add the bay leaf. Cover and simmer for 20 minutes.

3. Remove the bay leaf. Turn off the heat and stir in the heavy cream. Gradually add the cheese, one small handful at a time, stirring until each handful is melted before adding the next handful.

4. Stir in the Worcestershire and ground pepper. If the soup is not hot, return to low heat until warmed through.

5. Top with the croutons and, if desired, cracked pepper.

CREAMY PEA SOUP

This beautiful green soup was created by James Beard Award-winning Chef Sandy D'Amato, founder of Milwaukee's Sanford Restaurant. The restaurant is regarded by culinary experts as one of the Midwest's best. The sweetness of the peas and saltiness of the ham are a natural combination, with whole milk imparting velvety creaminess.

4   tablespoons butter

1   medium yellow onion, thinly sliced

2   celery stalks, thinly sliced

2   medium carrots, peeled and thinly sliced

4   leeks, cleaned and sliced* (white and light green parts only)

5   garlic cloves, crushed

5   cups chicken broth

¼   teaspoon dried thyme

2   bay leaves

4   cups frozen peas

3   cups milk

¼   teaspoon salt

¼   teaspoon freshly ground black pepper

¼   teaspoon ground nutmeg

1½ cups diced cooked ham

Croutons

1. Melt the butter in a stockpot over medium heat. Add the onion, celery, carrots, leeks, and garlic. Cook until softened, 10 to 15 minutes, stirring occasionally. Add the chicken broth, thyme, and bay leaves. Bring to a boil. Turn the heat to low and cover. Simmer for 20 to 25 minutes, or until the carrots are tender.

2. Remove the bay leaves and add the peas. Bring to a boil. Turn the heat to low and simmer, uncovered, until the peas are cooked, 2 to 3 minutes. Pour in the milk. Season with salt, pepper, and nutmeg. Let the soup cool slightly.

3. Transfer the soup to a blender in batches. (Do not fill the blender more than halfway.) Purée until smooth and creamy. Return the puréed soup to the stockpot. Add the ham and heat the soup over medium-low until heated through. Ladle soup into bowls and top with croutons.

*TIP To clean leeks, cut them in half lengthwise. Wash under cold running water, fanning the layers to remove dirt and grit. Shake then pat dry with clean paper towels; thinly slice.

GARDEN VEGETABLE SOUP

For a conversation-starter or ABC quiz with kids, stir 1 cup cooked alphabet pasta into the soup after it's cooked. If you're in a hurry, substitute 2 cups mixed frozen vegetables for the broccoli florets. And for a heartier soup, stir in 2 cups cooked cubed chicken breast along with the milk-flour mixture. To make this a veggie-cheese soup, stir in 1 cup shredded Cheddar cheese after the milk mixture has been added and the soup has thickened slightly.

2	tablespoons butter
1	small yellow onion, chopped
1	large potato, peeled and cubed
2	large carrots, peeled and thinly sliced
1	(14.5-ounce) can chicken broth
2	cups broccoli florets or 1-inch pieces green beans
1	teaspoon salt
1/4	teaspoon freshly ground black pepper
1/4	cup all-purpose flour
2 1/2	cups milk
	Pinch cayenne pepper (optional)

1. Melt the butter in a large saucepan over medium heat. Add the onion and cook until softened, about 5 minutes. Add the potato and carrots and continue to cook for another 5 minutes.

2. Pour in the broth and bring to a boil over high heat. Reduce the heat and simmer for 5 minutes.

3. Add the broccoli, salt, and pepper and simmer for another 5 minutes or until the vegetables are tender.

4. Place the flour in a small bowl and slowly whisk in the milk until combined and smooth. Pour the milk mixture into the soup and stir thoroughly. Simmer for another 5 minutes until the soup has thickened. If desired, add a pinch of cayenne pepper.

CLAM CHOWDER

Although this recipe comes from the fifth-generation Crandall Dairy Farm in Battle Creek, Michigan—far from chowder's East Coast roots—anyone who tastes it would be hard-pressed to argue against its deliciousness. Larry and Gloria Crandall and their sons, Brad and Mark—together with their wives—care for 240 dairy cows. While purists may think twice about topping chowder with cheese—and with bacon—it only makes it better! If you like, use smoked Cheddar or Gouda for an additional layer of smoky flavor in the chowder.

4 slices bacon

1 medium yellow onion, chopped

⅓ cup all-purpose flour

1 (8-ounce) bottle clam juice

2 (6.5-ounce) cans minced clams, drained, juice reserved

2 medium russet potatoes, scrubbed and diced

2 bay leaves

¼ teaspoon dried thyme, crushed

1 cup heavy cream

⅓ cup chopped fresh parsley

Salt

Freshly ground black pepper

½ cup shredded Cheddar cheese

1. Cook the bacon in a large saucepan over medium-low heat until crisp. Transfer to a paper towel–lined plate to drain.

2. Cook the onion in the bacon drippings over medium-low heat until softened, about 5 minutes. Add the flour and cook and stir for about 1 minute. Whisk in the bottled clam juice, the reserved juice from the canned clams, and 1 cup water. Bring to a boil, then lower the heat to maintain a simmer. Add the potatoes, bay leaves, and thyme. Simmer, covered, until the potatoes are tender, about 10 minutes.

3. Add the clams, cream, and parsley then simmer, uncovered, for another 2 minutes. Season to taste with salt and pepper.

4. To serve, crumble the bacon. Ladle the chowder into bowls and sprinkle with the crumbled bacon and cheese.

CREAMY VEGETABLE BARLEY SOUP

Frank Scibelli may be one of the most respected restaurateurs in Charlotte, North Carolina, but his success hasn't discouraged him from creating the kind of homey food (such as the recipe for this chunky soup) that he grew up cooking and eating in a food-loving Italian family. Most vegetable-barley soups are broth-based. The addition of whole milk—slightly thickened with cornstarch—makes this soup heartier.

1 (15-ounce) can chili beans, undrained

½ cup frozen corn kernels

½ cup medium pearl barley

1 (14.5-ounce) can fire-roasted diced tomatoes, undrained

1 cup sliced white mushrooms

1 cup chopped onion

1 carrot, peeled and sliced

1 stalk celery, sliced

3 garlic cloves, minced

2 teaspoons dried Italian seasoning, crushed

½ teaspoon salt

¼ teaspoon freshly ground black pepper

1 (14-ounce) can low-sodium chicken broth

¼ cup cornstarch

3 cups milk

¼ cup chopped fresh parsley

¼ cup grated Parmesan cheese

1. Combine the beans, corn, barley, tomatoes, mushrooms, onion, carrot, celery, garlic, Italian seasoning, salt, and pepper in a 3½ to 5-quart slow cooker. Pour the broth over all and stir to combine. Cover and cook on low for 8 to 9 hours or on high for 4 to 5 hours.

2. Near the end of the cooking time, whisk the cornstarch into the milk. Stir the milk mixture into the slow cooker until well blended. (If the cooker is on low, turn it to high.) Continue cooking for 20 to 30 minutes or until the soup has thickened.

3. To serve, ladle the soup into bowls. Sprinkle each serving with fresh parsley and Parmesan cheese.

TIP This soup is conveniently made in the slow cooker, so you can get it going then go about your day. If you'd like to make it on the stove (as shown in the photo, opposite), sauté the onion, mushrooms, celery, carrot, garlic, Italian seasoning, salt, and pepper in 2 tablespoons vegetable oil in a soup pot for 5 to 6 minutes or until crisp-tender. Stir in the beans, corn, barley, tomatoes, and broth. Cover and cook until the barley is tender, 30 to 40 minutes. Whisk the cornstarch into the milk, then stir into the soup. Let simmer, stirring frequently, for 5 minutes or until the soup is slightly thickened and creamy. Sprinkle each serving with fresh parsley and cheese.

JERSEY

EASY KEEPERS While there are some good-natured arguments among farmers, these soft brown cows with the big dark eyes and white muzzle may be considered the prettiest of dairy cows. Smaller than other breeds, their weight averages 1,000 pounds. Farmers who raise them say the Jersey's small stature is an advantage: They're easier to manage and feed. The Jersey's average annual milk production is almost 2,000 gallons, and its rich butterfat content increases the milk's value. The milk from Jersey cows contributes to creamy butter, Swiss cheese, and cottage cheese. In fact, each Jersey's annual milk production equals more than a ton of Cheddar cheese, according to the American Jersey Cattle Association.

STRENGTHS Based on the amount of milk produced per pound of feed consumed, Jerseys

stack up well in relation to other dairy breeds. Farmers appreciate the value of the Jersey's high

protein and butterfat production. And Jersey cows are noted for being tolerant to heat, which

is desirable in parts of the country where high temperatures are common.

ORIGIN British isle of Jersey. The first Jerseys came to the United States in the 1850s.

"WOW" COW One Jersey, Norse Star Hallmark Bootie, produced almost 4,700 gallons of milk.

Her owners at Norse Star Jerseys in Westby, Wisconsin, say she lives on through many offspring.

Her whole family is known for producing milk that is very rich in butterfat, says Jason

Fremstad of Norse Star Jerseys. "We like Jerseys for the fact that they are modest in size and

easy to handle. Even the calves are smaller, and a lot of kids use them for their first show

animals. My own kids are just getting to that age, and they will be showing Jerseys."

HOT HAM AND CHEESE SANDWICHES

A savory spread of butter, Dijon mustard, onion, toasted sesame seeds, and Worcestershire sauce gives these simple hot sandwiches great flavor. They can be made ahead and stored, wrapped in foil, in the refrigerator up to twelve hours before baking.

4	tablespoons butter, softened
1	tablespoon Dijon mustard
2	tablespoons finely chopped onion
1	tablespoon sesame seeds, toasted
1½	teaspoons Worcestershire sauce
6	onion or poppyseed hamburger buns
1¼	pounds thinly sliced deli ham
12	slices Swiss cheese

1. Preheat the oven to 350°F. Combine the butter, mustard, onion, sesame seeds, and Worcestershire sauce in a small bowl. Stir until smooth.

2. To assemble sandwiches, spread the butter mixture on the cut surfaces of the bun tops and bottoms. Evenly divide the ham among the six bottom buns. Top each pile of ham with two slices of cheese and a bun top. Wrap each sandwich in aluminum foil and place on a baking sheet.

3. Bake for 20 to 25 minutes, or until the cheese is melted and the sandwiches are warmed through. Serve warm.

CHEESE-STUFFED TURKEY BURGERS

Be sure to tightly seal the edges of the two patties together or the cheese will ooze out during grilling. Serve these deliciously gooey burgers with sweet potato oven fries.

¼ cup plain yogurt
¼ cup medium or hot salsa
1¼ pounds ground turkey
3 tablespoons yellow cornmeal
1 large egg, lightly beaten
½ teaspoon seasoned salt
2 teaspoons chili powder
4 slices Monterey Jack cheese with jalapeño peppers
   Bibb lettuce leaves
4 hamburger buns, toasted
4 thin slices red onion

1. Preheat a grill to medium-high. Stir the yogurt and salsa together in a small bowl. Cover and refrigerate until serving time.

2. Combine the turkey, cornmeal, egg, salt, and chili powder in a large mixing bowl. Divide the mixture evenly into eight ¼-inch-thick patties.

3. Top four of the patties with a slice of the cheese, tearing the cheese in pieces to fit if necessary. Cover with the remaining four patties then press the edges tightly together to seal.

4. Grill the patties for 5 to 6 minutes on each side. To assemble the burgers, place a lettuce leaf on each bun bottom. Top with a cooked patty, the salsa mixture, and sliced onion. Close each with the top of a bun.

TOASTED ITALIAN CHICKEN SUBS

Frozen fully cooked chicken breast fillets are available in the freezer section of most supermarkets. If you can't find them, broil four small (four- to five-ounce) chicken breast halves until cooked through, turning them halfway through the cooking time. Delicately flavored Provolone melts beautifully.

4   Italian rolls, split

2   tablespoons butter, softened

4   frozen fully cooked chicken breast fillets

2   cups pizza sauce, plus additional for serving

8   slices provolone cheese

Pepperoncini pepper rings

1. Preheat the oven to 350°F. Line a large rimmed baking sheet with aluminum foil. Butter the cut sides of the rolls, tops and bottoms, with the softened butter. Arrange, buttered sides up, on the prepared baking sheet; set aside.

2. Place the chicken breast fillets in a large microwave-safe bowl. Pour the pizza sauce over the chicken. Cover and microwave on high for 3 minutes, rearranging the chicken and stirring the sauce halfway through the cooking time.

3. Place a chicken breast fillet on the bottom of each roll. Cut or tear each slice of provolone in half and arrange four halves on top of each chicken breast. Top with pepperoncini rings to taste.

4. Bake for 20 to 25 minutes or until the cheese is melted and starting to bubble and brown. Top with the toasted roll tops and serve immediately with additional warmed pizza sauce.

CRUNCHY TURKEY WRAPS

These curried turkey wraps are handy for on-the-go meals. They can be made hours ahead and don't require any plates or forks—just a napkin or two. Greek yogurt provides a creamy, tangy base for the curried sauce that's studded with sweet and chewy raisins.

½ cup plain Greek yogurt

¼ cup raisins

½ teaspoon curry powder

4 whole wheat tortillas

1 cup shredded Cheddar cheese

8 ounces sliced turkey breast

1 cup fresh baby spinach

½ cup shredded carrots

1. Combine the yogurt, raisins, and curry powder in a medium bowl then mix until thoroughly blended.

2. To assemble the wraps, lay each tortilla on a flat work surface. Spread about 2 tablespoons of the yogurt mixture evenly on each tortilla, leaving a ½-inch border. Top with ¼ cup of the cheese, one-quarter of the turkey, ¼ cup of the spinach, and 2 tablespoons of the carrots. Roll up tightly then wrap tightly with plastic wrap. Chill for at least 1 hour before serving.

MONTEREY JACK PITA PIZZA

Made with chicken instead of Canadian bacon, this riff on classic Hawaiian pizza with pineapple is a quick-to-fix meal for two. For a lip-tingling twist, use Monterey Jack with jalapeño peppers instead of Monterey Jack.

1   (6-inch) pita bread

1   tablespoon pizza or pasta sauce

½   cup shredded Monterey Jack cheese

½   cup chopped cooked chicken breast

½   cup diced fresh pineapple

1   green onion, sliced

1. Preheat the oven to 375°F.

2. Carefully split the pita bread in half, separating it into 2 thin crusts. Arrange the pita halves on a baking sheet.

3. Spread the sauce evenly on each half. Divide the cheese between the halves.

4. Scatter the chicken and pineapple evenly over the cheese. Sprinkle with the green onion.

5. Place the baking sheet in the oven and bake for 8 to 10 minutes or until the cheese has melted and the edges are browned.

Apple-Cheddar Pizza, page 74

APPLE-CHEDDAR PIZZA

The combination of tart apples, sweet raisins, salty ham, and sharp Cheddar cheese makes for wonderfully balanced flavor on this autumnal pizza (see page 72). (Serve with a sprinkle of crushed red pepper if you like a little heat.) It makes a warming midday meal or—cut in small squares—a tasty appetizer for a party.

Nonstick cooking spray

4 tablespoons butter

2 Granny Smith apples, peeled (if desired), cored, and coarsely chopped

¼ teaspoon dried thyme, crushed

¼ teaspoon freshly ground black pepper

1 tablespoon fresh lemon juice

2 tablespoons raisins

2 tablespoons sugar

1 (13.8-ounce) tube refrigerated pizza dough

¼ cup slivered almonds, toasted

⅓ cup diced ham

2 green onions, sliced

1 cup shredded sharp Cheddar cheese

1. Preheat the oven to 425°F. Spray a nonstick baking sheet with cooking spray; set aside.

2. Melt the butter in a skillet over medium heat. Add the apples, thyme, and pepper and cook just until tender, 5 minutes. Add the lemon juice, raisins, and sugar and continue cooking until the juices thicken slightly, 1 to 2 minutes. Using a slotted spoon, transfer the apple mixture to a bowl, reserving the juices in the skillet.

3. Unroll the pizza dough onto the prepared baking sheet and press into a 9-by-14-inch rectangle. Spread the apple mixture evenly over the dough. Drizzle with the reserved cooking juices from the skillet. Sprinkle with the almonds, ham, and green onions. Top with the cheese.

4. Bake for 12 to 14 minutes or until the crust is golden brown and the cheese is melted.

FRIDAY NIGHT PIZZA PARTY
Cucumber Yogurt Dip with veggie dippers (page 112)
Apple-Cheddar Pizza
Wild Mushroom Pizza with Roasted Garlic Purée (page 75)
Monterey Jack Pita Pizza (page 71)
Buttermilk Brownies (page 191)

WILD MUSHROOM PIZZA
WITH ROASTED GARLIC PURÉE

Chef John Caputo is a fixture of the Chicago restaurant scene. He developed a pizza featuring slow-cooked garlic, wild mushrooms, and Fontina cheese while heading the kitchen at Bin 36, a wine-centric restaurant with an earthy yet elegant menu. This is a close adaptation of that restaurant version, slightly simplified for home cooks. Fontina originated in Italy and is now made in this country as well. It has a slightly nutty flavor and buttery texture that melts beautifully, a natural for pizza.

GARLIC PURÉE

- 2 large heads garlic
- 2 tablespoons olive oil, divided
- 1 tablespoon sherry vinegar
- ¼ to ½ teaspoon salt
- ¼ teaspoon freshly ground black pepper

PIZZA

- 1 tablespoon olive oil
- 1 tablespoon coarse-ground cornmeal
- All-purpose flour
- 1 pound prepared pizza dough, at room temperature
- ¾ cup grated mozzarella cheese
- ¾ cup grated Fontina cheese
- 1½ cups sliced mushrooms (such as shiitake, cremini, and/or white button)
- ¼ cup chopped hazelnuts

1. For the garlic purée, preheat the oven to 400°F. Remove any loose papery skins from garlic heads. Cut a ½ inch off the narrow end to expose the cloves. Place the garlic heads on a piece of aluminum foil. Drizzle with 1 tablespoon of the olive oil. Wrap up tightly and bake for 45 to 50 minutes or until garlic is soft and golden; let cool. Turn the oven temperature to 450°F.

2. Squeeze the garlic pulp into a small bowl. Add the remaining 1 tablespoon olive oil, the sherry vinegar, salt, and pepper. Stir and mash with a fork until smooth; set aside.

3. For the pizza, grease a 14-inch round pizza pan with the olive oil. Sprinkle with the cornmeal; set aside.

4. On a lightly floured surface, roll the pizza dough into a 14-inch circle. Place in the prepared pizza pan, stretching to fit as needed. Spread the garlic purée evenly over the dough, leaving a ¼-inch border around the edge. Sprinkle the cheeses evenly over the purée. Top with the mushrooms and hazelnuts.

5. Bake for 12 to 15 minutes or until the crust is golden brown and the cheese is melted.

EASY CHEESY CALZONE

These appealing pocket sandwiches provide a perfect way to get kids to eat broccoli—smothered with cheese and pepperoni and dipped in warm pizza sauce. The recipe is versatile too. Swap some of the broccoli for chopped red or yellow bell peppers or mushrooms—or sliced green olives for the black ones.

Nonstick cooking spray

All-purpose flour

1 (13.8-ounce) tube refrigerated pizza dough

1 (14.4-ounce) package frozen broccoli cuts (4½ cups)

2 cups shredded mozzarella cheese

¼ cup shredded Parmesan cheese

¼ cup sliced black olives

⅓ cup mini pepperoni slices or chopped pepperoni

Pizza sauce, warmed

1. Preheat the oven to 400°F. Spray a nonstick baking sheet with nonstick cooking spray.

2. Lightly flour a work surface and roll the pizza dough to form a 10-by-14-inch rectangle, about ¼ inch thick. Transfer the dough to the prepared baking sheet.

3. Cook the broccoli in a covered dish in the microwave on high for 6 minutes, stirring once halfway through cooking. Drain. Snip any large pieces with clean kitchen scissors; set aside.

4. Scatter half the mozzarella cheese on one half of the dough, leaving a ½-inch border. Sprinkle with the Parmesan cheese. Scatter the broccoli on the cheese. Top the broccoli with the remaining mozzarella, the black olives, and pepperoni.

5. Fold unfilled dough over the filling and seal the edges with a fork. Prick the top several times to allow steam to escape.

6. Bake for about 20 minutes or until the crust is lightly browned. Cool for 5 minutes on a rack before slicing. Serve with warm pizza sauce.

THREE-CHEESE BEEF AND VEGGIE CALZONES

Although traditional calzones are made into half-moon shapes, these quick and easy calzones call for a tube of refrigerated pizza dough, which makes it easy to cut into quarters for rectangular calzones. They look different but still taste just like a calzone should. The most popular Italian cheeses—provolone, mozzarella, and Parmesan—join forces for authentic flavor.

Nonstick cooking spray

1 tablespoon extra-virgin olive oil

1 small red onion, halved and thinly sliced

1 cup sliced white button mushrooms

2 cups packed baby spinach leaves, coarsely chopped

¼ teaspoon crushed red pepper flakes

Freshly ground black pepper

All-purpose flour

1 (13.8-ounce) tube refrigerated pizza dough

8 ounces thinly sliced deli roast beef

¼ cup sun-dried tomatoes, chopped

2 slices provolone cheese, cut in half

½ cup shredded mozzarella cheese

4 (1-inch) strips jarred roasted red peppers

4 tablespoons grated Parmesan cheese

Pizza sauce, warmed (optional)

1. Preheat the oven to 350°F. Lightly spray a rimmed baking sheet with nonstick cooking spray.

2. Heat the olive oil in a skillet over medium heat. Add the onion and mushrooms and cook until the onions are softened and lightly browned, about 5 minutes. Add the spinach and stir just until it wilts, about 1 minute. Season with the crushed red pepper and black pepper to taste. Remove from the heat and allow to cool to room temperature, about 15 minutes.

3. Meanwhile, to assemble the calzones, lightly flour a work surface. Unroll the dough and cut it into four pieces. Roll each piece into a 6-by-8-inch rectangle.

4. For each calzone, place one-quarter of the roast beef on one half of the rectangle, leaving a ½-inch border. Top with one-quarter each of the sun-dried tomatoes, the provolone and mozzarella cheeses, and the cooled vegetable mixture. Top with a strip of roasted red pepper and 1 tablespoon of the Parmesan cheese. Fold dough in half over the filling then press the edges with a fork to seal. Carefully transfer the calzones to the prepared baking sheet.

5. Bake on the middle rack of the oven for 20 to 25 minutes or until browned and heated through. Let stand for 10 minutes. Serve with warm pizza sauce, if desired.

BARBECUE PORK TACOS

Southern barbecue meets Mexican fare in this lightning-fast midday meal. You'll have some coleslaw left after putting part of it in the tacos. Serve it as a side or save it for another meal—it keeps well in the refrigerator up to two days.

1 (16-ounce) bag coleslaw mix

¾ cup prepared coleslaw dressing

1 (16-ounce) tub prepared shredded barbecued pork

12 (6-inch) corn tortillas (yellow or white)

3 cups shredded Monterey Jack cheese with jalapeño peppers

Barbecue sauce (optional)

1. Preheat the oven to 350°F.

2. Combine the coleslaw mix and dressing in a large bowl. Toss to coat well; refrigerate until ready to serve.

3. Heat the barbecued pork in the microwave according to the package directions.

4. Arrange the tortillas in a single layer on two large baking sheets. Heat in the oven until warmed, 2 to 3 minutes.

5. Place 2 to 3 tablespoons of the pork in the center of each tortilla. Return to the oven for 1 to 2 minutes. Top with the shredded cheese and coleslaw. Serve immediately, with additional coleslaw on the side and additional barbecue sauce, if desired.

CONFETTI QUESADILLAS

A colorful profusion of vegetables and black beans fills these cheesy quesadillas served with a side of creamy cilantro-yogurt dip. If you're making this for grown-ups who like spicy food, leave some of the seeds in the jalapeño before chopping it.

CILANTRO–YOGURT DIP

- 1 cup plain Greek yogurt
- ¼ cup finely chopped fresh cilantro
- ½ teaspoon ground cumin

QUESADILLAS

- 1 (10-ounce) package 6-inch soft corn tortillas (12 tortillas)
- 1 (8-ounce) package shredded Colby Jack cheese blend (2 cups)
- ½ cup corn kernels
- ½ cup black beans
- ½ cup coarsely chopped fresh cilantro
- 1 red bell pepper, finely chopped (1 cup)
- 1 jalapeño pepper, seeded and finely chopped

1. For the cilantro-yogurt dip, stir together the yogurt, cilantro, and cumin in a small bowl; set aside.

2. For the quesadillas, preheat the oven to 300°F. Lay six tortillas on a work surface. Divide the cheese, corn, beans, cilantro, and peppers among the tortillas. Cover each with a second tortilla.

3. Place one quesadilla in a dry nonstick skillet over medium-high heat. Cook for 4 to 6 minutes, turning once halfway through the cooking time, or until the cheese is melted and the tortillas are slightly golden. Remove the quesadilla from the skillet and place on a baking sheet in the oven to keep warm. Repeat with the remaining quesadillas.

4. Cut the quesadillas into wedges. Serve with a dollop of the cilantro-yogurt dip.

QUICK CHICKEN ENCHILADAS WITH YOGURT SAUCE

Leftover cooked chicken breast makes these creamy enchiladas simple to get on the table on even the busiest days. Melted cream cheese stirred together with salsa and shredded Mexican cheese blend imparts the chicken filling with savory deliciousness.

ENCHILADAS
Nonstick cooking spray

4 ounces cream cheese

2 cups chopped cooked chicken breast

1 (16-ounce) jar green or red salsa (2 cups), divided

1½ cups shredded Mexican cheese blend, divided

8 (6-inch) flour tortillas

YOGURT SAUCE
1 cup plain Greek yogurt

¼ cup chopped fresh cilantro

½ teaspoon ground cumin

1. For the enchiladas, preheat the oven to 350°F. Spray a 9-by-13-inch baking dish with nonstick cooking spray.

2. Heat the cream cheese in a medium-size nonstick skillet over medium-low heat until softened. Stir in the chicken and ½ cup of the salsa and stir until combined. Add ½ cup of the cheese and stir until melted.

3. Spoon about ¼ cup of the chicken mixture onto each tortilla then roll up. Place the filled enchiladas, seam sides down, in the prepared baking dish. Top with the remaining 1½ cups salsa. Cover with aluminum foil and bake for 15 minutes. Remove the foil and sprinkle the enchiladas with the remaining 1 cup cheese. Bake, uncovered, for another 5 to 10 minutes or until cheese is melted and bubbling.

4. For the yogurt sauce, whisk the yogurt, cilantro, and cumin in a medium bowl. Cover and chill until ready to serve.

5. To serve, top the enchiladas with a dollop of the yogurt sauce.

BEEF BURRITOS WITH PEPPER JACK CHEESE AND BLACK BEANS

Precooked rice and canned beans give you a jump-start on these chunky burritos. All you have to do is cook some ground beef, roll up the fillings, and zap them in the microwave for one minute until the cheese is melted and the burritos are heated through.

Nonstick cooking spray

½ pound lean ground beef

2 garlic cloves, minced

1 cup salsa, plus additional for serving

1 (8.8-ounce) pouch precooked brown or white rice, or 2 cups cooked brown or white rice

1 (15-ounce) can black beans, rinsed and drained

1 (11-ounce) can corn kernels, drained

6 (10-inch) flour tortillas

2 cups shredded Monterey Jack cheese with jalapeño peppers

⅓ cup sliced green onions, white and green parts (about 2)

1. Spray a medium-size nonstick skillet with nonstick cooking spray. Brown the ground beef and garlic in the skillet over medium heat for 5 to 7 minutes. Drain the fat and stir in ½ cup of the salsa; set aside.

2. Heat the rice in its pouch according to the package directions (or heat cooked rice in the microwave on high for 1 minute to separate the grains) and transfer to a medium mixing bowl. Add the beans and corn to the rice and mix well.

3. Spread about 1 cup of the rice mixture on a tortilla just below the center (closest to you), leaving a 1-inch border. Spread about ⅓ cup of the beef on the rice mixture. Top with about ⅓ cup cheese, then with a generous tablespoon of salsa and some of the green onions. Fold the bottom of the tortilla over the filling. Fold in the sides of the tortilla over the filling. Roll up from the bottom, completely enclosing filling. Place, seam side down, on a microwave-safe plate. Repeat with the remaining tortillas and filling.

4. Heat the burritos, one at a time, on high in the microwave for 1 minute or until heated through. Serve with additional salsa.

BLACKENED FISH TOSTADAS WITH WATERMELON SALSA

Use just about any white-fleshed fish you like in these spicy-sweet tostadas. The recipe calls for tilapia, but sole, cod, catfish, halibut, or flounder work equally well. These fish varieties vary in thickness, though, so be sure the fish is thoroughly cooked. Watermelon and feta cheese are frequent culinary partners. The tangy, salty cheese—with its firm texture—is a nice contrast to the sweet juiciness of the melon.

SALSA

- 2 cups seedless watermelon, cut into ½-inch cubes
- ¼ cup chopped red onion
- 2 tablespoons fresh lime juice
- ¼ cup minced fresh cilantro

FISH

- 4 tablespoons blackening spice blend
- 4 (5-ounce) tilapia fillets
- 2 tablespoons canola oil

TOSTADAS

- 2 cups shredded cabbage
- 2 medium tomatoes, chopped (about ¾ cup)
- 2 ripe avocados, pitted, peeled, and cubed
- 8 corn tostadas
- ½ cup crumbled feta cheese

1. For the salsa, gently toss the watermelon, onion, lime juice, and cilantro together in a large bowl. Cover with plastic wrap and refrigerate until serving, up to 1 hour.

2. For the fish, sprinkle 1 tablespoon of the blackening spice evenly on both sides of each fillet. Heat the oil in a large nonstick skillet over medium-high heat. Add two fillets and cook for 3 to 4 minutes on each side until cooked through. Transfer to a plate and keep warm. Repeat with the remaining two fillets.

3. For the tostadas, divide the cabbage, tomatoes, and avocados among the eight tostadas. Top each tostada with half a fish fillet and about ¼ cup of the watermelon salsa. Sprinkle each with 1 tablespoon of the feta cheese and serve immediately.

TURKEY BURRITOS WITH CHEDDAR

With a filling of celery, sweet potato, stuffing mix, and turkey, these burritos make good use of Thanksgiving leftovers. Include the optional jalapeño for a spicy twist. Use mild or sharp Cheddar, depending on your preference.

1 tablespoon butter

1 cup chopped onion (1 medium)

2 cups diced peeled sweet potato (1 medium)

⅓ cup diced celery (1 stalk)

1 (14.5-ounce) can chicken broth

¼ teaspoon freshly ground black pepper

2 cups cubed cooked turkey breast

1 cup dry stuffing mix

1 jalapeño pepper, seeded and minced (optional)

4 (10-inch) flour tortillas (burrito-size)

2 cups shredded Cheddar cheese

Salsa verde, for serving

1. Melt the butter in a nonstick skillet over medium heat. Cook the onion, sweet potato, and celery, covered, in the butter until the vegetables are crisp-tender, about 4 minutes. Pour in the broth and add the black pepper. Bring to a boil; reduce the heat and simmer until the vegetables are soft, about 4 minutes.

2. Add the turkey and stuffing mix and continue to cook, uncovered, for 5 minutes, stirring frequently, until the filling is heated through and has thickened. Stir in the minced jalapeño, if using.

3. To assemble the burritos, place a tortilla on a work surface and top with ½ cup of the cheese and one-quarter of the filling (about 1 cup). Fold the bottom of the tortilla over the filling. Fold in the sides of the tortilla over the filling. Roll up from the bottom, completely enclosing filling. Place, seam side down, on a plate. Repeat with the remaining tortillas and filling.

4. If desired, microwave the burritos, one at a time, for 30 seconds to melt the cheese and warm them through. Serve with salsa verde.

RITA'S EASY QUICHE

Rita Kennedy runs Kennedy Farm with her husband, James, in Valencia, Pennsylvania. Rita says she is always looking for meals that are quick and easy and that call for "lots of dairy products." Her family, she says, loves anything with "lots of cheese." This biscuit-crusted quiche fits the bill.

Nonstick cooking spray

3 large eggs

1½ cups milk

½ cup biscuit mix

6 tablespoons butter, melted and cooled slightly

¼ teaspoon salt

¼ teaspoon freshly ground black pepper

½ cup diced ham or cooked crumbled bacon

1 cup sliced fresh mushrooms

¼ cup thinly sliced green onion or chopped yellow onion

1 cup shredded Swiss cheese

1. Preheat the oven to 350°F. Spray a 9-inch pie pan or glass pie plate with nonstick cooking spray; set aside.

2. Beat the eggs lightly in a medium mixing bowl. Add the milk, biscuit mix, butter, salt, and pepper. Whisk until smooth. Pour into the prepared pan. Sprinkle with the ham, mushrooms, and green onion. Top with the cheese.

3. Bake for 40 to 45 minutes or until puffed and golden brown. Let stand for 10 minutes before serving.

Cows enjoy their meals and aren't troubled in the least if the food service is sometimes more industrial than pastoral. Modern dairy farms range from small to large—and every size in between.

CHEESY CHICKEN CRUNCHERS

These chicken fingers have an extra dose of yum—shredded Cheddar cheese in the cornflake coating! Serve with your favorite bottled barbecue sauce for a quick kid-friendly meal.

Nonstick cooking spray

1 cup all-purpose flour

½ teaspoon salt

½ teaspoon freshly ground black pepper

4 large egg whites

½ cup milk

3 cups cornflakes, crushed

1½ cups shredded Cheddar cheese

1½ pounds boneless, skinless chicken breasts

Bottled barbecue sauce

1. Preheat the oven to 375°F. Spray a nonstick baking sheet with nonstick cooking spray; set aside.

2. Combine the flour, salt, and pepper in a shallow dish. In a second dish, whisk the egg whites and milk. In a third dish, combine the cornflakes and cheese.

3. Pat the chicken breasts dry with paper towels. Cut them into 1-inch-wide strips. Dip each piece first in the flour, then in the egg mixture, and finally in the cornflake mixture. Place the coated chicken pieces on the prepared baking sheet. When all the chicken pieces are coated, spray them with the nonstick cooking spray.

4. Bake for 20 to 25 minutes, or until the chicken is cooked through and the coating is golden-brown and crisp. Serve warm with your favorite barbecue sauce for dipping.

CURRY CHICKEN SALAD

Next time you bake chicken breasts for supper, add a couple of extra breasts to the pan so you can make this crunchy chicken salad for the next midday meal. Tiny cubes of mozzarella are stirred into this mix, but you could also use a mild Swiss or Havarti, if you like.

¾ cup diced mango

¾ cup plain yogurt

1 to 1¼ teaspoons curry powder

2 (6-ounce) packages cooked chicken breast strips, or 12 ounces cooked chicken breast, cut into bite-size pieces

⅓ cup dried sweetened cranberries

⅓ cup coarsely chopped walnuts

½ cup diced mozzarella cheese

2 green onions, sliced

½ cup sliced celery

8 Bibb lettuce leaves

1. Combine the mango, yogurt, and curry powder in a blender. Blend until smooth; set aside.

2. Combine the chicken, cranberries, walnuts, cheese, green onions, and celery in a large mixing bowl. Pour the curry dressing over the chicken mixture and stir gently to combine. Chill for 1 hour to allow the flavors to blend.

3. Arrange two lettuce leaves on each serving plate. Divide the chicken salad among the plates on top of the lettuce.

Meet No. 3937 and her posse. Cows are social animals, enjoying the company of their peers. And they're genuinely curious if someone shows up with something new, like a camera.

"We like raising our kids in a way that they learn hard work and responsibility. It's great being around them on the farm." —Gregg Knutsen, Delaware dairy farmer

GREGG & STEPHANIE KNUTSEN HARRINGTON, DELAWARE

For dairy farmer Gregg Knutsen, the thrill is in genetics, raising cows that are stronger and healthier than their ancestors. He and Stephanie, along with children Bethany, Evan, and Emmie, own and operate G&S Dairy near Harrington, Delaware. They enjoy showing cattle at the county, regional, and national levels, and their cows often stand tall in the show ring.

"We've had several cows win high honors in shows and fairs, including the Maryland and Delaware state fairs," says Gregg. "One of our best cows is called Alma. She just scored an excellent for the Holstein breed."

That ranking means she achieved high scores for body type, structure, and other physical traits on which dairy cows are judged. Alma isn't just a beauty; she backed up her show-ring ranking with production of more than 4,200 gallons of milk in the same year.

"Showing cattle at a competitive event is like a horse show or dog show," says Gregg. "We love the animals and we like to show them off. I think it's a good measure of how well you take care of the animals. When they are well cared for, they look good and feel good, and that means they produce a quality product for consumers. It all ties together."

Their sixty-cow herd of Holstein and Jersey cows is not large, but some of the award-winning G&S genetics are found in cows on many other farms across the country. They have several cows that have done well in the show ring and also have excellent production records.

"When you show cattle, you have to train them to lead on a halter, and that builds trust between the animal and the person," says Gregg.

"We love being dairy farmers," he adds. "I like working with the cows, but it's more than that. Stephanie and I like raising our kids in a way that they learn hard work and responsibility. It's great being around them on the farm."

See Stephanie's recipe for Hot Cheesy Potatoes on page 170.

STEAK AND ARUGULA SALAD WITH WALNUT DRESSING

When summer grilling season arrives, serve up this hearty salad of peppery greens, tomatoes, and butter-roasted potatoes. A homemade dressing made with walnuts, Dijon mustard, and Greek yogurt—and a topping of blue cheese—takes it from good to great.

DRESSING

- ½ cup coarsely chopped walnuts
- ¼ cup white vinegar
- ¼ cup plain Greek yogurt
- 2 teaspoons Dijon mustard
- ½ teaspoon salt
- ½ teaspoon freshly ground black pepper
- ¼ cup walnut oil

SALAD

- ½ cup coarsely chopped walnuts
- Nonstick cooking spray
- ¾ pound new potatoes, quartered
- 2 tablespoons butter, melted
- Salt
- Freshly ground black pepper
- 1½ pounds sirloin steak, about 1 inch thick
- 4 cups packed arugula leaves
- 2 cups cherry or grape tomatoes, halved
- 1 cup crumbled blue cheese

1. Preheat the oven to 375°F. Preheat a grill to medium-high.

2. For the dressing, combine the walnuts, vinegar, yogurt, mustard, salt, and pepper in a blender. Blend on high speed until smooth. With the blender running, slowly add the walnut oil and blend for another 5 seconds. Transfer the dressing to a small bowl. Cover and refrigerate until ready to serve.

3. For the salad, spread the walnuts on a baking sheet. Toast in the oven until light golden brown, about 4 minutes, stirring once; set aside to cool. Leave the oven on.

4. Spray a large rimmed nonstick baking sheet with nonstick cooking spray. Toss the potatoes with the melted butter in a medium bowl. Season to taste with salt and pepper. Transfer the potatoes to the prepared baking sheet. Roast for 20 to 30 minutes or until browned and tender, stirring once or twice.

5. Meanwhile, season the steak to taste with salt and pepper. Grill for 5 to 7 minutes per side, to your desired doneness. Remove the steak from the grill. Let rest for 5 minutes, then thinly slice.

6. To assemble the salad, toss the arugula and tomatoes in the dressing. Divide among four serving plates. Top with the steak, potatoes, blue cheese, and toasted walnuts. Serve immediately.

POMEGRANATE SPINACH SALAD

Pomegranates are in season from early fall to midwinter. If you can find the seeds (also called arils) already taken out of the fruit, it will save time making this salad. It is a nice side to a sandwich or a bowl of soup—or a main-dish salad by adding leftover chicken breast or pork chop to the plate. A generous dose of Parmesan imparts nutty, buttery flavor to the salad.

SALAD

¾ cup pomegranate seeds (1 pomegranate)

1 (9-ounce) bag fresh baby spinach

1 red onion, thinly sliced (about 1½ cups)

1 (8-ounce) package fresh, white mushrooms, sliced (about 2 cups)

1 cup shredded Parmesan cheese

DRESSING

¼ cup canola oil

3 tablespoons apple cider vinegar

2 tablespoons sugar

¼ teaspoon paprika

2 teaspoons poppy seeds

1. For the salad, first remove the seeds from the pomegranate: Fill a large bowl with cool water. Cut the pomegranate in half and place in bowl. With the fruit under water, gently remove the seeds. The waxy pulp will rise to the top. Scoop the pulp out with a small strainer and discard. Drain and gently pat the seeds dry on a paper towel.

2. Toss together the pomegranate seeds, spinach, onion, mushrooms, and Parmesan cheese in a very large serving bowl.

3. For the dressing, combine the oil, vinegar, sugar, and paprika in a blender. Blend until smooth. Pour into a small bowl and whisk in the poppy seeds.

4. Pour the dressing over the salad. Toss well and serve immediately.

PEAR SALAD

This simple and pretty composed salad can be made just about anywhere. The ingredients—canned pears, lettuce, shredded Cheddar, mayo, and maraschino cherries—are portable and easily stored in a cooler for picnics and camping trips.

1 (15-ounce) can pear halves

4 iceberg or Boston lettuce leaves

1 cup shredded Cheddar cheese

4 tablespoons mayonnaise

4 maraschino cherries (with or without the stems)

1. Place one pear half on each lettuce leaf (save any remaining pears for another use). Top each with ¼ cup of the cheese, 1 tablespoon mayonnaise, and 1 cherry. Serve immediately.

TIP Assemble each salad individually on serving plates or all of the salads on a large serving platter for pretty presentation.

A dairy farm often includes generations of a farm family and many descendants of a great dairy cow. A Holstein heifer may be prized because her great-grandmother was an outstanding producer or lived a long and healthy life.

AFTER-CHORES
snacks

DIPS · NIBBLES · DRINKS
FROZEN TREATS

RECIPES

ARTICHOKE AND ROASTED RED PEPPER YOGURT DIP

This dip made with Greek yogurt comes from Jay and Kristy Ackley, dairy farmers from East Liberty, Ohio. They farm 2,800 acres and have a herd of about 110 dairy cows. "I always say that Jay and I were blessed with two sons and one hundred girls that we take care of," Kristy says. The dip can be ready and waiting in the fridge for an anytime snack. Chill it at least three hours or overnight to allow the flavors—garlic, cayenne, and green onions—to infuse the dip.

1   cup jarred roasted red peppers, drained and chopped

1   (14-ounce) jar marinated artichoke hearts, drained and chopped

2   cups plain Greek yogurt

¼   teaspoon salt

⅛   to ¼ teaspoon cayenne pepper

2   garlic cloves, minced

⅓   cup chopped green onions, white and green parts (about 2)

    Pita chips or tortilla chips, for serving

1. Pat the roasted red peppers and artichoke hearts dry with paper towels.

2. Combine the red peppers, artichokes, yogurt, salt, cayenne, garlic, and green onions in a medium bowl and stir until well blended. Transfer to a serving bowl. Cover and refrigerate at least 3 hours or overnight to allow the flavors to blend.

3. Serve with pita chips or tortilla chips.

BAKED SPINACH-ARTICHOKE YOGURT DIP

There seems to be some version of this popular dip at nearly every potluck party. With a yogurt base—rather than more commonly used mayonnaise—this one is lighter and healthier.

Softened butter, for the baking dish

1 (14-ounce) can artichoke hearts, drained and chopped

1 (10-ounce) package frozen chopped spinach, thawed and squeezed dry

1 cup plain yogurt

1 cup shredded mozzarella cheese

1 cup grated Parmesan cheese

¼ cup thinly sliced green onions, white and green parts

1 garlic clove, minced

¼ cup chopped red bell pepper

Pita chips, tortilla chips, crackers, and/or toasted baguette slices

1. Preheat the oven to 350°F. Butter a 1-quart casserole dish or 9-inch glass pie plate; set aside.

2. Combine the artichokes, spinach, yogurt, mozzarella, Parmesan, green onions, garlic, and bell pepper in a large bowl; mix thoroughly.

3. Transfer to the prepared dish. Bake for 30 to 35 minutes or until bubbling and lightly browned on top. Let stand for 5 minutes. Serve with pita chips, tortilla chips, crackers, and/or toasted baguette slices for dipping.

START TO FINISH: 10 minutes **MAKES:** 6 servings

PB&C DIP

A little bit of honey adds a touch of sweetness to this dip. Leave it out if you prefer it less sweet. The combination of peanut butter and cottage cheese provides a powerful protein punch.

- **1 cup 4% milkfat cottage cheese**
- **2 tablespoons peanut butter**
- **¼ teaspoon ground cinnamon or apple pie spice**
- **1 tablespoon honey**
- **1 teaspoon milk, plus more as needed**
- **3 medium apples or pears, cored and sliced**

1. Combine the cottage cheese, peanut butter, cinnamon, honey, and milk in a blender or food processor. Cover and blend or process until smooth. If necessary, add milk until the dip reaches the desired consistency.

2. Serve the dip immediately or cover and chill up to 24 hours. Serve with apple and/or pear slices for dipping.

"Every day is Earth Day when you make your living off the land." —John Koepke, Wisconsin dairy farmer

JOHN & KIM KOEPKE OCONOMOWOC, WISCONSIN

The city has come to the farm for Koepke Family Farms of Oconomowoc, Wisconsin. When John Koepke's great-great-grandfather settled there in 1875 and began a dairy farm, thoughts of the city were far away. But in 140 years, greater Milwaukee has come to the front door.

Waukesha County used to have 60,000 dairy cows and a few thousand people; today there are 400,000 people and only 2,800 cows.

John and Kim's farm (operated in partnership with John's dad and uncle) is one of the largest remaining, with 330 Holsteins. "We're on the front yards of lots of people," says John. "We work hard to be understanding of all our neighbors and put our best foot forward."

One way they do this is by meeting their neighbors at area farmers' markets, where they sell their locally produced cheese and other dairy products. Another is how they treat their farmland, with terraces—a series of graduated steps of land—and other measures to reduce soil erosion. They rotate crops to conserve natural resources. "Diversity is good for the soil," says John. Over the years, the farm has won numerous soil conservation awards. That's not only good for their farm, it's also good for their relationships with neighbors.

The Koepkes' Holsteins produce some eye-popping numbers. One cow, Granny, lived to be more than twenty years old and produced a whopping 53,300 gallons of milk in her lifetime, a world record. "I guess you could say our cows are like our family—built to last," says John.

"We love what we do here on our farm," he says. "We work outside with our family, with the cows, and with the land. We produce a food we're proud of. Every day is Earth Day when you make your living off the land."

PREP: 5 minutes **CHILL:** 1 hour **MAKES:** 12 servings

CREAMY APPLE BUTTER DIP

Kids will love this lightly spiced dip made with cream cheese, apple butter, and peanut butter. It's delicious with apples or graham crackers, but try it with celery too. Diane Hoover of Brook-Corner Holsteins in Lebanon, Pennsylvania, invented it when her local dairy promotion committee needed a dairy snack to serve at an apple festival. "Visitors kept coming back for more!" she says.

- 1 (8-ounce) package cream cheese, softened
- 1 cup apple butter
- 1 cup creamy peanut butter
- Apple slices, pear slices, and/or graham crackers

1. Beat the cream cheese, apple butter, and peanut butter with an electric mixer on medium speed in a medium bowl until smooth. Cover with plastic wrap and refrigerate for 1 to 4 hours before serving.

2. Serve with apple and pear slices and/or graham crackers for dipping.

BROWN SWISS

THE OLD STALWARTS These big brown cows rank second when it comes to producing milk, averaging about 2,200 gallons of milk a year per cow. They are noted for their sturdiness and durability. Brown Swiss are one of the most populous breeds worldwide, with herds in the United States most concentrated in Iowa, Ohio, and Wisconsin. Kids tend to love Brown Swiss for their floppy ears and docile temperament.

STRENGTHS Brown Swiss cows produce milk with high butterfat and protein content, which appeals to butter and cheese-makers. The cows are noted for their tolerance of a wide range of weather conditions and ability to thrive when grazing.

ORIGIN The mountaintops of northeast Switzerland. Some historians believe they are the

oldest dairy breed, dating back to 4000 B.C. They were brought to the United States in 1869.

"WOW" COW Snickerdoodle is perhaps the most famous Brown Swiss and easily the most decorated. She's owned by Allen Basler of Old Mill Farm in Upperville, Virginia. Snickerdoodle has been the Grand Champion of her breed six times at the World Dairy Expo in Wisconsin, the only cow of any breed to accomplish this feat. She also has been the Supreme Champion (best dairy cow of all breeds) at the Expo, and she finished second overall two other years.

"Snickerdoodle just has this incredible bloom about her," says Allen, who raised her from a calf. "She's sixteen years old, but she carries herself like she's six." Her line continues not only on her home farm but also in milking herds across the country.

CUCUMBER YOGURT DIP

This twist on tzatziki—Greek yogurt dip—calls for the addition of softened cream cheese for a bit of extra richness. Served with a bounty of bright, beautiful vegetables, this dip makes a healthful snack and is pretty for a party.

1	cup plain Greek yogurt
4	ounces cream cheese, softened
½	small cucumber, peeled, seeded, and diced small
1	garlic clove, minced
1	teaspoon fresh lemon juice
¼	teaspoon freshly ground black pepper
1	tablespoon chopped fresh dill
2	tablespoons finely chopped fresh mint
	Vegetables for dipping, such as carrots, celery, radishes, zucchini, snap peas, and/or bell pepper strips

1. Mix the yogurt and cream cheese together in a medium bowl until smooth. Add the cucumber, garlic, lemon juice, pepper, dill, and mint then blend thoroughly. Chill for at least 1 hour or until serving time.

2. Serve with vegetables for dipping.

Despite being herd animals, cows can have very distinct personalities and individual preferences. A dairy farm may spend a great deal on shade, which most of the herd appreciates, but there's always one who thinks she'd rather stretch out for a bit of sunbathing.

SALMON TORTILLA ROLLS

Chef Kathy Cary of Lilly's Bistro in Louisville, Kentucky, makes a warm grilled version of these smoky cream cheese–and–salmon-filled bites. In this slightly tweaked recipe, the rolls can be made ahead, chilled, and served at a moment's notice.

1   avocado, pitted, peeled, and diced small

2   teaspoons fresh lime juice, divided

1   (8-ounce) package cream cheese, softened

4   ounces smoked salmon, chopped

1   tablespoon finely chopped chipotle chile in adobo sauce

¼   cup sliced green onions

3   (10-inch) flour tortillas

3   cups chopped romaine lettuce

1   cup diced tomato

1. Gently toss the avocado and 1 teaspoon of the lime juice in a small bowl; set aside.

2. Combine the cream cheese, the remaining 1 teaspoon lime juice, the salmon, chipotle, and green onions in a medium bowl. Gently mix until well combined.

3. Spread about one-third of the cream cheese mixture evenly on one tortilla. Layer with about one-third of the lettuce, one-third of the tomato, and one-third of the avocado. Roll up tightly. Wrap in plastic wrap and set aside.

Repeat with the remaining cream cheese mixture, tortillas, lettuce, tomato, and avocado. Refrigerate the rolls for 1 to 4 hours.

4. To serve, trim the ends of the rolls to be even (about a ½ inch off each end). Slice each roll into eight pieces. Serve immediately.

Orange Cream Chiller (with bananas), page 118

Orange Cream Chiller (with strawberries), page 118

Vanilla Iced Mochaccino,
page 116

Shamrock Milk Mixer,
page 117

VANILLA ICED MOCHACCINO

This refreshing, invigorating coffee drink (see page 115) tastes like one you can get in a coffee shop, but at a fraction of the cost—and you can have it anytime you like! Be sure to use whole milk for the richest, creamiest taste and texture.

2 cups strong brewed coffee

1 cup milk

1 tablespoon unsweetened
   cocoa powder

1 tablespoon sugar

1 teaspoon vanilla extract

1. Combine the coffee, milk, cocoa powder, sugar, and vanilla extract in a small saucepan over medium heat. Bring to a simmer; simmer for 5 minutes. Let cool for 5 minutes.

2. Pour the coffee mixture over ice into two large cups with lids or into one large cocktail shaker. Shake well. (If using a cocktail shaker, pour into two ice-filled 16-ounce glasses before serving.) Serve immediately.

Mutual curiosity gets satisfied as this boy pets the forehead of a Holstein. The cow must enjoy the interaction as she has to stretch her head down and forward to accommodate the youngster's reach.

SHAMROCK MILK MIXER

This bright green, pistachio-flavored treat (see page 115) gives you an excuse to crumble a cookie into your milk. (It's yummy with a cookie on the side, too.) Store any unused pudding mix in an airtight container.

1 cup cold milk

2 tablespoons pistachio-flavored instant pudding and pie filling mix

1 chocolate-mint sandwich cookie, crushed*

1. Pour the milk into a tall glass. Add the instant pudding mix and stir with a fork to dissolve. Stir in the crushed cookie. Serve immediately.

*TIP Place the cookie in a small plastic bag and crush it with a rolling pin or with your hands.

A veterinarian gets acquainted with youngsters in her care. Like human children, calves are susceptible to common childhood illnesses. Checkups and attentive care ensure that they'll grow into healthy, productive cows.

ORANGE CREAM CHILLER

Third-generation dairy farmers Lad and Brenda Hastings and their two young boys cool down with this dreamsicle-style treat (see page 114) after chores on their dairy farm in Geauga County, Ohio. Hastings Dairy—also home to the Hastings' own Rowdy Cow Creamery—hosts tours for schools, camps, seniors, and service groups so anyone can learn about "cows and milk production from farm to table." This double dose of dairy in the form of milk and yogurt provides both protein and calcium.

3 ounces frozen orange juice concentrate, thawed

1 cup milk

½ cup plain Greek yogurt

1 small frozen banana, or 3 frozen strawberries

1 teaspoon honey

½ teaspoon vanilla extract

1. Combine the orange juice concentrate, milk, yogurt, frozen banana, honey, and vanilla in a blender. Blend on high until smooth.

2. Divide between two 12-ounce glasses. Serve immediately.

VANILLA EGGNOG

Bill and Merri Post of Middleroad Acres in Chandler, Minnesota, are among those who have adopted "milking robots" that assist in milking their 120 Holsteins. The Posts came to a realization a few years ago that they had to update their process or sell their cows, which Bill said he "could not imagine." The milking barn isn't the only place the Posts use technology. Fans of their Facebook page find all kinds of delicious recipes posted by Merri for sharing—such as this freshly made eggnog.

3   pasteurized large eggs, or ¾ cup pasteurized egg product, such as Egg Beaters*

⅓   cup sugar

4   cups cold milk

1   cup vanilla yogurt

1   teaspoon vanilla extract

⅛   teaspoon salt

Freshly grated nutmeg, for garnish

1. Combine the eggs, sugar, milk, yogurt, vanilla extract, and salt in a blender. Cover and blend until frothy. Divide among six 8-ounce serving glasses and garnish with freshly grated nutmeg.

*TIP It's important to use either pasteurized eggs or pasteurized egg product in this recipe to ensure the quality and safety of the drink.

This calf nurses eagerly from a bottle, which can provide her with the necessary nutrients to grow.

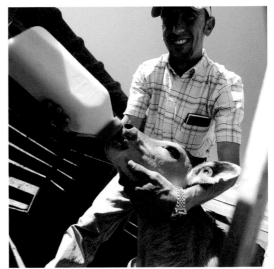

DOUBLE STRAWBERRY MILKSICLES

These old-fashioned frozen treats are cool, creamy goodness. Make them as a fun activity for kids (with a little help from a grown-up) on a hot summer day. Frozen strawberries and strawberry frozen yogurt give them a pretty pink hue.

1 (10-ounce) package frozen strawberry halves in syrup

1 cup milk

½ cup strawberry frozen yogurt

12 (3-ounce) plastic or paper cups and 12 wooden craft sticks or 12 (2-ounce) freezer pop molds

1. Partially thaw the strawberries by leaving them at room temperature for 10 minutes or microwaving the unopened plastic pouch on high for 10 seconds.

2. Place the partially frozen berries with their liquid in a blender. Add the milk and frozen yogurt. Cover and blend until smooth. Divide among twelve cups or freezer pop molds. Place the cups in a 9 by 13-inch baking pan. Cover each cup with aluminum foil. Push a craft stick through the center of the foil to hold the stick in place while freezing. Freeze until firm, 3 to 4 hours.

DOUBLE BLUEBERRY MILKSICLES Substitute one (10-ounce) package frozen blueberries in syrup for the frozen strawberry halves. Substitute blueberry frozen yogurt for the strawberry frozen yogurt. Makes 12 servings.

CREAMY VANILLA MILKSICLES Omit the frozen strawberry halves. Increase the milk to 1½ cups. Substitute 1 cup vanilla frozen yogurt for the ½ cup strawberry frozen yogurt. Add 1 teaspoon vanilla extract. Makes 12 servings.

CARAMELICIOUS MILKSICLES

These milksicles are fun to make. Kids will love swirling the caramel ice cream topping through the creamy milk mixture. If you're short on time, try the quick version.

⅓ cup sugar

2 tablespoons cornstarch

1½ cups milk

1½ teaspoons vanilla extract

⅓ cup caramel ice cream topping, at room temperature

6 (3-ounce) plastic or paper cups and 6 wooden craft sticks or 6 (2-ounce) freezer pop molds

1. Combine the sugar and cornstarch in a medium saucepan. Gradually whisk in the milk. Bring to a boil over medium-high heat. Lower the heat and simmer until thickened, about 2 minutes, whisking frequently.

2. Remove from the heat; stir in the vanilla extract. Transfer to a large shallow bowl. Chill in the refrigerator for 40 minutes, stirring occasionally.

3. Drop heaping teaspoons of the caramel ice cream topping randomly over the chilled milk mixture. Lightly swirl the caramel into the milk mixture.

4. Spoon the mixture into six cups or freezer pop molds. Place the cups in an 8 by 8-inch baking pan or pie pan. Cover each cup with foil. Push a craft stick through the center of the foil to hold the stick in place while freezing. Freeze until firm, 3 to 4 hours.

SHORTCUT METHOD
Substitute instant vanilla pudding mix for the sugar, cornstarch, milk, and vanilla in the main recipe. Make the pudding according to the package directions, swirling the caramel ice cream topping into the finished pudding. Proceed with the freezing instructions. Makes 6 servings.

CARAMEL PUDDING VARIATION After swirling in the caramel topping, divide the mixture among four dessert dishes. Cover each dish with plastic wrap and chill in the refrigerator until serving time. Serve chilled. Makes 4 servings.

TAIL WAGGIN' DOG BISCUITS

Your best buddy deserves a treat after helping out with chores—even if that means just keeping you company. These Parmesan-and–peanut butter biscuits from Heins Family Farms are sure to elicit a very enthusiastic response! Fifth-generation dairy farmers Paul and Cindy Heins—together with their son Chris—milk 650 Holsteins at their Higgonsville, Missouri, farm.

Nonstick cooking spray
1 cup all-purpose flour
1 tablespoon chicken bouillon granules, or 1 bouillon cube, crushed
1 teaspoon baking powder
¼ cup grated Parmesan cheese
2 tablespoons peanut butter
1 large egg white
½ cup milk

1. Preheat the oven to 400°F. Lightly spray a large nonstick baking sheet with nonstick cooking spray; set aside.

2. Combine the flour, bouillon granules, baking powder, cheese, and peanut butter in a medium bowl. Stir to combine (mix with your fingers, if necessary). Whisk the egg white and milk in a small bowl until combined. Add to the dry ingredients and stir to combine.

3. Using a tablespoon, drop the batter by the spoonful onto the prepared baking sheet. Bake for 10 to 15 minutes or until golden brown. Cool on a wire rack.

Farm dogs have jobs to do, whether it's keeping a watchful eye on the dairy herd or on the family's children. Homemade dog biscuits seem like the perfect reward for either responsibility.

SUNDOWN
supper

POULTRY · MEAT · FISH
PASTA AND RICE · CASSEROLES · SALADS AND SIDES

RECIPES

TWO-CHEESE MEDITERRANEAN STUFFED CHICKEN

These stuffed chicken breasts are elegant enough to serve to company. Summer Vegetable Risotto (page 156) makes a perfect side dish.

3 tablespoons olive oil, divided

½ cup chopped onion

1 cup diced tomatoes

1 large garlic clove, minced

1 (6-ounce) bag baby spinach

1 cup shredded mozzarella cheese

¼ cup shredded Parmesan cheese

4 medium boneless, skinless chicken breast halves (about 1¾ pounds)

2 teaspoons Italian seasoning blend, crushed

Salt

Freshly ground black pepper

1. Preheat the oven to 350°F.

2. Heat 2 tablespoons of the oil over medium heat in a skillet. Cook the onion in the hot oil, stirring, until tender, about 5 minutes. Stir in the tomatoes and garlic. Add the spinach; cover and cook just until the spinach is wilted, about 3 minutes. Remove from the heat and let the mixture cool to room temperature, about 15 minutes. Drain any excess juices from the vegetables.

3. Add the mozzarella and Parmesan cheeses to the vegetables. Stir until all the ingredients are well combined.

4. Using a sharp knife, cut a pocket in each chicken breast half by cutting horizontally through the thickest portion to, but not through, the opposite side. Pack one-quarter of the filling into each breast half. Press lightly on the top of each breast to close the opening as tight as possible.

5. Arrange the stuffed breasts in a 9 by 13-inch baking dish. Brush the tops of the chicken breasts with the remaining 1 tablespoon oil. Season with the Italian seasoning, salt, and pepper to taste.

6. Bake for 30 minutes or until a thermometer inserted into the center of a breast reaches 165°F. Let stand for 5 to 10 minutes before serving.

PARMESAN CHICKEN FETTUCCINE

No one walks away from the table hungry when Chris Sukalski serves this very tasty one-dish supper to her husband and three teenagers. Chris also serves as the dairy manager for Reiland Farms in LeRoy, Minnesota, where she is in partnership with her brother, Scott Reiland, caring for a 400-cow milking herd. Chris does a lot of public speaking and leads tours at her farm to help consumers understand modern dairy production and to experience all it has to offer.

1 pound fettuccine

3 cups small fresh broccoli florets

¾ cup (1½ sticks) butter, divided

¾ teaspoon salt, divided

½ teaspoon freshly ground black pepper, divided

12 ounces boneless, skinless chicken breasts, cut into bite-size pieces

1 small onion, chopped

2 garlic cloves, minced

4 ounces fresh mushrooms, sliced

3 cups whipping cream

1½ cups grated Parmesan cheese, plus additional for serving

6 slices bacon, cooked and crumbled, divided

Cracked black pepper

1. Cook the fettuccine according to the package directions, adding the broccoli in the last 3 minutes of cooking; drain and keep warm.

2. Meanwhile, melt 2 tablespoons of the butter in a large skillet over medium heat. Season the chicken with ½ teaspoon of the salt and ¼ teaspoon of the ground pepper. Cook in the hot butter until cooked through, 5 to 6 minutes. With a slotted spoon, transfer the chicken from the skillet to a plate; set aside. Add 2 tablespoons of the butter to the skillet. Cook the onion, garlic, and mushrooms in the hot butter just until the vegetables are softened, 4 to 5 minutes. Set aside.

3. Combine the remaining ½ cup (1 stick) butter and the heavy cream in a medium saucepan over medium-low heat. Heat and stir until the butter is melted, about 2 minutes. Stir in the remaining ¼ teaspoon salt and remaining ¼ teaspoon ground pepper. Add the Parmesan cheese and stir until the cheese is melted. Stir in the chicken, onion mixture, and half the bacon.

4. Toss the drained pasta and broccoli with the chicken mixture. Divide among six serving plates. Top with additional grated Parmesan, the remaining bacon, and cracked pepper.

OVEN-BBQ CHICKEN AND CHEDDAR VEGGIE PACKETS

Whether you're camping, tailgating, or simply eating at home, this one-dish supper can conveniently be made ahead of time. Assemble and refrigerate the packets up to eight hours before cooking. Serve with extra barbecue sauce on the side.

4 (6 to 8-ounce) boneless, skinless chicken breast halves

¼ cup barbecue sauce, plus additional for serving

4 small red potatoes, thinly sliced

1 green or red bell pepper, seeded and sliced into 8 rings

½ cup thinly sliced green onions, white and green parts

Salt

Freshly ground black pepper

2 cups shredded Cheddar cheese

1. Preheat the oven to 375°F. For each packet, place a sheet of heavy-duty aluminum foil, about 12 by 12 inches, on a work surface. Place one chicken breast half in the center of the foil. Brush 1 tablespoon of the barbecue sauce over the chicken. Top with one sliced potato, two bell pepper rings, and 2 tablespoons sliced green onion. Season to taste with salt and black pepper.

2. Bring the two opposite sides of the foil together and fold down, sealing tightly. Roll up the short ends of the packet to seal tightly. Place the packet on a large rimmed baking sheet. Repeat with the remaining ingredients.

3. Bake for 35 minutes. Carefully open each packet with scissors and peel back the foil. Sprinkle ½ cup of the cheese on each serving. Return to the oven for 2 to 3 minutes, or until the cheese has melted.

4. Place one packet on each serving plate (or carefully slide the contents onto the serving plate). Serve with additional barbecue sauce, if desired.

TURKEY-VEGETABLE CASSEROLE

This artichoke-studded rice casserole, flavored with Havarti cheese and bacon, finds a good home for leftover roasted turkey or chicken.

Softened butter, for the baking dish

- 1 tablespoon butter
- ½ cup chopped carrot
- ½ cup chopped celery
- ¼ cup sliced green onions, white and green parts
- 1 (10.75-ounce) can condensed cream of chicken soup
- 1 (14-ounce) can artichoke hearts, drained and coarsely chopped
- 1½ cups chopped cooked turkey or chicken (8 ounces)
- 1½ cups cooked long grain and wild rice blend (unseasoned)
- 1 cup shredded Havarti cheese
- ⅔ cup milk
- ½ teaspoon dried thyme, crushed
- ¼ teaspoon dried sage leaves, crushed
- ¼ teaspoon freshly ground black pepper
- 4 slices bacon, cooked until crisp, drained, and crumbled
- ¼ cup grated Parmesan cheese
- Sliced green onions, for garnish (optional)

1. Butter a 2-quart baking dish. Preheat the oven to 350°F. Melt the butter in a large saucepan over medium heat. Cook the carrot, celery, and green onions in the hot butter until the carrot is crisp-tender, about 6 minutes. Remove from the heat. Stir in the soup, artichokes, turkey, rice, Havarti, milk, thyme, sage, pepper, and bacon. Transfer to the prepared baking dish. Sprinkle with the Parmesan cheese.

2. Cover and bake for 20 minutes. Uncover and bake for about 20 minutes more or until bubbly. Let stand for 10 minutes before serving. Sprinkle with additional green onions, if desired.

Granny's Chicken Pie, page 138

GRANNY'S CHICKEN PIE

When dairy farmer Barbara Sink Myers was growing up in the 1950s in Lexington, North Carolina, she remembers the congregation of the Shiloh Methodist Church holding chicken pie suppers to finance the building of a new church. One Saturday a month, one family would be in charge of cooking, but the entire congregation pitched in to help. "I have fond memories of cooking with family and friends, pouring sweet tea, waiting tables, and greeting customers," Barbara says. "These suppers were a lot of hard work, but I will always cherish the feeling of love, fellowship, and the sense of belonging built by this united effort." (Recipe pictured on page 136.)

⅓ cup butter

1 small onion, chopped

½ cup sliced celery

⅓ cup all-purpose flour

1¾ cups chicken broth

⅔ cup milk

¼ teaspoon salt

¼ teaspoon freshly ground black pepper

1 (14.1-ounce) package refrigerated pie crust (2 crusts)

2 cups diced cooked chicken

2 hard-cooked eggs, chopped

1. Preheat the oven to 425°F. Melt the butter in a stockpot over medium heat. Cook the onion and celery in the hot butter until the onion is soft and translucent, 5 to 6 minutes. Whisk in the flour and cook for 1 minute. Slowly add the chicken broth and milk and whisk until smooth. Season with the salt and pepper. Simmer over medium-low heat until thickened, 2 to 3 minutes. Remove from the heat and set aside to cool slightly.

2. Unroll one pie crust and place it in a 9-inch pie plate. Place the chicken in the bottom crust. Sprinkle the chopped eggs over the chicken. Pour the broth mixture over the chicken and eggs.

3. Top with the second crust. Trim to make the edges even, if necessary. Turn the edges under to seal the crust. Crimp and flute the edges to make a rim. Cut slits in the top crust to allow steam to escape.

4. Place the pie on a rimmed baking sheet and bake for 30 to 35 minutes or until the crust is nicely browned and the filling is bubbling. Let stand for 20 minutes on a wire rack before serving.

PORK TENDERLOIN WITH ROASTED ROOT VEGETABLES AND MUSHROOM CREAM

This dish has special-occasion flavor without special-occasion fussiness. Serve it with steamed fresh green beans tossed with butter and toasted almonds.

VEGETABLES

¾ pound baby Yukon Gold or red potatoes, quartered

1 medium parsnip, peeled and cut into 1-inch chunks

1 medium carrot, peeled and cut into 1-inch chunks

2 tablespoons extra-virgin olive oil

Salt

Freshly ground black pepper

PORK

1 (1- to 1½-pound) pork tenderloin

½ teaspoon salt

¼ teaspoon ground black pepper

½ teaspoon dried thyme, crushed

2 tablespoons vegetable oil

MUSHROOM CREAM

1 tablespoon butter

1½ cups sliced mushrooms

½ cup dry white wine

1 (8-ounce) package cream cheese, cut into chunks

¼ cup milk

2 tablespoons Dijon mustard

Freshly ground black pepper

1. Preheat the oven to 400°F. For the vegetables, place the vegetables on a rimmed baking sheet and toss with the olive oil. Season to taste with salt and pepper. Place the baking sheet in the oven and roast for 30 to 35 minutes or until golden brown and tender, stirring once or twice.

2. For the pork, pat the tenderloin dry with a paper towel. Season with the salt, pepper, and thyme. Heat the vegetable oil in a large ovenproof skillet over medium-high heat. When the oil is very hot, place the pork in the skillet and brown on all sides, about 6 minutes.

3. Transfer the skillet to the oven and roast for 15 to 20 minutes or until a thermometer inserted in the thickest part of the tenderloin reaches 145°F. Remove the pork from the oven and cover with aluminum foil. Allow to rest for 10 minutes. Carve into ¾-inch slices.

4. Meanwhile, for the mushroom cream, melt the butter in a small saucepan over medium heat. Sauté the mushrooms in the hot butter until lightly browned and tender, about 5 minutes. Add the wine and cream cheese. Turn the heat to low and stir until the cream cheese is melted. Whisk in the milk and mustard. Season to taste with pepper. Heat through.

5. To serve, arrange the vegetables on a serving platter and top with the pork. Pour the mushroom cream over all. (Or divide the vegetables and pork among four plates and top with mushroom cream.)

APRICOT-DIJON PORK CHOPS WITH POTATO PANCAKES AND HERBED SOUR CREAM

As you cook the pancakes, place them on a paper towel–lined baking sheet in a 200°F oven to keep them warm as you cook the remaining batter.

PORK CHOPS

Nonstick cooking spray

⅓ cup apricot preserves

2 tablespoons coarse-ground Dijon mustard

4 (1-inch-thick) boneless pork top loin chops (about 1½ pounds total)

½ teaspoon salt

½ teaspoon freshly ground black pepper

PANCAKES

½ cup sour cream

1 tablespoon snipped fresh chives

2 teaspoons snipped fresh dill

1 medium sweet potato, peeled

1 large russet potato, peeled

2 green onions, very thinly sliced

2 large eggs, lightly beaten

3 tablespoons all-purpose flour

1 tablespoon freshly squeezed lemon juice

½ teaspoon salt

¼ teaspoon freshly ground black pepper

1 tablespoon butter

Snipped fresh dill and chives, for garnish

1. For the pork chops, lightly spray a broiler pan with nonstick cooking spray; set aside. Preheat the broiler to high. For pork chop glaze, stir the preserves and mustard together in a small saucepan. Warm over medium-low heat until blended and heated through. Snip any large pieces of fruit; set aside.

2. Season the pork chops with the salt and pepper. Broil 4 to 5 inches from the heat for 8 minutes on the prepared pan. Turn the chops. Brush generously with the apricot-mustard mixture. Broil for 5 minutes more or until the glaze starts to lightly char, the chops are cooked through, and a thermometer inserted into the center of a chop reads 145°F. Cover lightly with aluminum foil and let rest for 5 minutes.

3. For the herbed sour cream, stir together the sour cream, chives, and dill in a small bowl. Cover and chill until ready to serve.

4. For the pancake batter, shred the potatoes into a large bowl. Stir in the green onions, eggs, flour, lemon juice, salt, and pepper. Stir until well combined.

5. Melt the butter in a large nonstick skillet over medium heat. Using a generous ¼ cup for each pancake, drop the batter into the hot butter. Using a spatula, flatten each to 4 inches. Cook for 6 to 7 minutes or until golden brown and crisp and cooked through, turning once halfway through cooking. Drain the pancakes on a paper towel–lined baking sheet. Add more butter to the pan and continue cooking pancakes, stirring the between each batch. (You should get 8 pancakes.)

6. Top the warm pancakes with the herbed sour cream. Sprinkle the pancakes and chops with additional fresh dill and chives.

Cuban Tortas, page 144

CUBAN TORTAS

Citrus- and garlic-marinated pork shoulder is slow-cooked for hours, then shredded and stacked on toasty cheese rolls with crunchy shredded cabbage, spicy pickled jalapeños, and cilantro cream sauce (see page 142). It's perfect party food!

PORK
½ cup fresh lime juice
¼ cup orange juice
3 garlic cloves, minced
1 teaspoon dried oregano, crushed
1 teaspoon salt
½ teaspoon ground cumin
½ teaspoon freshly ground black pepper
2 bay leaves
1 3-pound boneless pork shoulder roast
1 medium onion, thinly sliced

CILANTRO CREAM SAUCE
1 cup sour cream
1 cup mayonnaise
½ cup finely chopped fresh cilantro
2 teaspoons lime peel
2 tablespoons fresh lime juice

SANDWICHES
8 to 10 bolillo or ciabatta rolls*
4 cups shredded Chihuahua or Monterey Jack cheese
1½ cups shredded green cabbage
½ cup sliced pickled jalapeño peppers

1. For the pork marinade, combine the lime juice, ¼ cup water, the orange juice, garlic, oregano, salt, cumin, black pepper, and bay leaves in a small bowl. Trim the fat from the meat. If necessary, cut it to fit into a 3½ to 5-quart slow cooker. Pierce the meat with a large fork in several places. Place in a large resealable plastic bag set in a deep bowl. Pour the marinade over the meat. Close the bag and chill in the refrigerator for 6 to 24 hours, turning occasionally.

2. Arrange the onion slices in the slow cooker. Place the meat on top of the onion. Pour the marinade over all. Cover and cook on low for 10 to 12 hours or on high for 5 to 6 hours.

3. Meanwhile, for the cilantro cream sauce, stir together the sour cream, mayonnaise, cilantro, lime peel, and lime juice in a small bowl. Cover tightly and refrigerate until serving time.

4. Transfer the meat to a large bowl or casserole and cool slightly. Skim any fat from the juices in the cooker. Remove and discard the bay leaves. Use two forks to shred the meat. Remove the onion from the slow cooker with a slotted spoon and add it to the meat in the bowl. Pour some of the warm juices over the meat and onion; cover and keep warm.

5. For the sandwiches, preheat the oven to 350°F. Slice each roll in half and place the cut side up on two large baking sheets. Divide the cheese among the roll halves. Bake until the cheese has melted and the bread is lightly toasted, 3 to 5 minutes.

6. Top the roll bottoms with the pork and onion, cabbage, jalapeños, and cilantro cream sauce. Top with the roll tops. Slice each sandwich in half and serve warm.

*TIP If you can't find either of these kinds of rolls, a crusty sub roll will work fine.

YOGURT-BAKED COD WITH PARSLEY PANKO CRUMBS

When students in a cooking class taught by Carla Hall—a *Top Chef* All Star and cohost of ABC's *The Chew*—were hesitant to try a French technique, Carla came up with the idea of using yogurt to create a creamy sauce (see page 146). "Thick and rich Greek yogurt works great," she says. "Just be sure to pull the fish out of the oven as soon as it's done—the yogurt will break if it's overcooked."

2 tablespoons plus 1 teaspoon butter, divided, plus more for the dish

1 cup panko bread crumbs

1 tablespoon olive oil

2 medium onions, thinly sliced

2 sprigs fresh thyme

Kosher salt

3 celery stalks, sliced ¼ inch thick at an angle

¼ cup plus 1 tablespoon dry white wine, divided

1 cup plain Greek yogurt, stirred

1 tablespoon fresh lemon juice

2 teaspoons Dijon mustard

1 teaspoon sugar

½ teaspoon freshly grated nutmeg

Freshly ground black pepper

6 (6-ounce) skinless, boneless center-cut cod fillets

1 teaspoon fresh lemon zest

¼ cup fresh flat-leaf parsley leaves, finely chopped

1. Preheat the oven to 350°F. Butter a shallow 2-quart casserole dish.

2. Melt 2 tablespoons of the butter in a small microwave-safe bowl. Add the bread crumbs and rub into butter until the crumbs are well coated. Spread the crumbs in a single layer on a rimmed baking sheet and bake until golden brown, about 5 minutes.

3. Heat the oil and remaining 1 teaspoon butter in a medium skillet over medium-low heat. Add the onions, thyme, and 1 teaspoon salt. Cook, stirring occasionally, until the onion is translucent, about 13 minutes. Increase the heat to medium and cook, stirring, until browned, about 3 minutes. Add the celery and cook, stirring, until bright green and still crunchy but no longer white in the center, about 3 minutes. Add ¼ cup of the wine and cook, stirring and scraping up the browned bits, until the liquid evaporates, about 2 minutes. Discard the thyme and transfer the mixture to the prepared dish.

4. Meanwhile, stir together the yogurt, lemon juice, mustard, sugar, nutmeg, the remaining 1 tablespoon wine, ½ teaspoon salt, and ¼ teaspoon pepper.

5. Season the fish with salt, then arrange the pieces over the onion mixture in a single layer, spacing the pieces apart. Pour the yogurt mixture over the fish. Bake until a thin-bladed knife easily slides through the fish, about 15 minutes.

6. Stir the lemon zest and parsley into the bread crumbs then sprinkle over the fish. Serve immediately.

Yogurt-Baked Cod with Parsley Panko Crumbs, page 145

SLOW-COOKED BEEF STROGANOFF

Coming home on a cold fall or winter night to the wonderful aroma of this hearty dish bubbling away in the slow cooker is comfort defined.

1½ pounds beef stew meat

1 tablespoon vegetable oil

2 cups sliced fresh mushrooms

½ cup sliced green onions or chopped yellow onion

2 garlic cloves, minced

½ teaspoon dried thyme, crushed

¼ teaspoon salt

¼ teaspoon freshly ground black pepper

½ teaspoon smoked paprika or paprika

1 bay leaf

1½ cups beef broth

⅓ cup dry sherry

1 (8-ounce) container sour cream

⅓ cup all-purpose flour

2 teaspoons snipped fresh dill, plus more for garnish

Cooked egg noodles

1. Cut up any large pieces of stew meat. Heat the oil in a large skillet over medium-high heat. Brown the meat, half at a time, in the hot oil. Drain off fat.

2. Combine the mushrooms, green onions, garlic, thyme, salt, pepper, paprika, and bay leaf in a 3½ or 4-quart slow cooker. Add the browned meat. Pour the beef broth and sherry over all.

3. Cover and cook on low for 8 to 10 hours or on high for 4 to 5 hours. Remove and discard the bay leaf.

4. If using the low heat setting, turn the heat to high. Whisk the sour cream, flour, and ¼ cup water in a medium bowl until smooth. Stir about 1 cup of the hot liquid from the slow cooker into the sour cream mixture. Return to the slow cooker and stir to combine. Cover and cook for about 30 minutes more or until thickened and bubbly.

5. Right before serving, stir in the fresh dill. Serve over noodles. Sprinkle with additional snipped fresh dill.

AYRSHIRE

EXCELLENCE IN MODERATION Ayrshires are admired for their beautiful mahogany coloring that varies from very light to very dark. In addition, irregular color patches can be scattered over the body. Ayrshire cows are of moderate size and each cow produces about 1,750 gallons of milk a year.

STRENGTHS Dairy farmers praise the breed's physical attributes and appreciate Ayrshires as excellent grazers that tend to live long and productive lives in a milking herd. To demonstrate the breed's stamina, in 1929 two cows were walked from the Ayrshire Association headquarters in Vermont to a national dairy show in St. Louis. Today, Ayrshires are most concentrated in Vermont, Connecticut, New York, Pennsylvania, Ohio, Wisconsin, Minnesota, and Iowa.

ORIGIN County of Ayr in Scotland. They came to the United States in the 1820s.

"WOW" COW Hawksfield Bronara is among the most productive Ayrshire of all time. Now twenty years old, she has produced more than 41,000 gallons of milk as a member of the herd. Her owner, Charles Sayles of Hawksfield Farm in Perry, Michigan, says several things make her special.

"She produced over 3,500 gallons one year as a young cow," he says. Her lifetime production records made her a five-time winner of the Lifetime Production Award from the Ayrshire Breeders Association, more wins than any other cow.

She has many daughters and granddaughters milking in herds in the United States and abroad. "We knew she was special when she was just a young cow," says Charles. "She's almost like a part of the family to us and is really fun to work with."

ROASTED SWEET POTATO EMPANADAS WITH GARLIC– RED PEPPER DIPPING SAUCE

Mashed sweet potatoes, two kinds of cheese, and peas are encased in a flaky, buttery crust in this Spanish-style supper. The dipping sauce is essentially Romesco—a smooth and savory sauce of puréed roasted red peppers, garlic, olive oil, and almonds.

EMPANADAS

- 2 **small sweet potatoes, peeled and quartered**
- 4 **tablespoons butter, divided**
- 1 **teaspoon salt**
- ¼ **teaspoon freshly ground black pepper**
- 1 **small sweet onion, chopped**
- ¼ **cup diced carrots**
- ¼ **cup crumbled blue cheese**
- ½ **cup shredded mozzarella cheese**
- ¼ **cup frozen peas, thawed**
  All-purpose flour
- 1 **(14.1-ounce) package refrigerated pie crusts (2 crusts)**
- 1 **large egg, lightly beaten**

SAUCE

- 1 **cup jarred roasted red peppers**
- 2 **garlic cloves**
- 2 **tablespoons unsalted almonds**
- ¼ **teaspoon salt**
- 2 **tablespoons extra-virgin olive oil**
- 2 **teaspoons red wine vinegar**

1. For the empanadas, preheat the oven to 400°F. Place the sweet potatoes on a rimmed baking sheet. Melt 3 tablespoons of the butter. Toss the potatoes with the melted butter, salt, and pepper until coated. Bake for 25 to 30 minutes or until browned and tender. Transfer the baking sheet to a wire rack and allow the potatoes to cool slightly. Leave the oven on.

2. Melt the remaining 1 tablespoon butter in a medium skillet over medium heat. Add the onion and cook until softened, 3 to 4 minutes. Add the carrots and continue cooking until the vegetables are very tender, 6 to 7 minutes more.

3. Mash the sweet potatoes in a large bowl. Stir in the cooked carrots and onions, blue and mozzarella cheeses, and the peas.

4. Lightly flour a work surface, then roll out one pie crust to a 13-inch circle. With a 5-inch round cookie cutter, cut out four rounds. Place 3 tablespoons of the potato filling in the center of each round. Moisten the edges of the dough lightly and fold the round over to create a half-moon shape. Press very lightly around edges to seal. Place the empanadas on a large nonstick baking sheet. Repeat with the remaining pie crust and filling. Brush the empanadas with the beaten egg.

5. Bake for 20 to 25 minutes or until golden brown.

6. Meanwhile, for the sauce, combine the red peppers, garlic, almonds, salt, olive oil, and vinegar in a blender. Cover and blend until smooth.

7. Serve the warm empanadas with the sauce.

Summer Vegetable Risotto, page 156

SUMMER VEGETABLE RISOTTO

Risotto has an undeserved reputation for being fussy. It requires a bit of stirring, but it is actually a simple dish to make. Three things contribute to its legendary creaminess—the starch that is released by the Arborio rice as it cooks and, of course, butter and cheese. (Recipe pictured on page 154.)

8 cups low-sodium chicken or vegetable stock

2 tablespoons butter

1 small yellow onion, finely chopped

2 cups Arborio rice

1 cup dry white wine

½ cup sliced asparagus (½-inch pieces)

½ cup diced zucchini

½ cup diced yellow squash

½ cup fresh or frozen peas

1 cup shredded Italian-style cheese blend

1 tablespoon snipped fresh thyme or basil

2 Roma tomatoes, seeded and diced

1 teaspoon kosher salt

½ teaspoon freshly ground black pepper, plus additional for serving

Cracked black pepper

½ cup shaved Parmesan

1. Bring the stock to a simmer in a large saucepan over medium heat. Turn the heat to low and keep hot but not boiling throughout the cooking process.

2. Melt the butter in another large saucepan over medium heat. Add the onion and cook until softened, 5 to 6 minutes.

3. Add the rice and stir to thoroughly coat. Add the wine and stir until the wine has almost evaporated. Add the stock, 1 cup at a time, stirring constantly until each cup is absorbed. (Turn the heat to low if necessary to keep at a constant low simmer.)

4. When the stock is nearly gone, add the asparagus, zucchini, yellow squash, and peas. Continue to cook, stirring frequently, until the liquid has been absorbed and the rice is tender but still slightly firm. (You may not use all of the stock. The risotto should be very creamy—not quite soupy, but almost.)

5. Gently stir in the Italian-style cheese and the thyme. Stir in the tomatoes. Add the salt and ground pepper. Serve immediately topped with cracked pepper and shaved Parmesan.

HAPPY BIRTHDAY! MENU

Pork Tenderloin with Roasted Root Vegetables and Mushroom Cream (page 139)

Summer Vegetable Risotto

Roasted green beans

Triple-Layer Chocolate Cake with Vanilla Buttercream (page 202)

PARMESAN ALFREDO VEGGIE SHELLS

Easy enough for a family supper but fancy enough for company, these stuffed shells baked in Parmesan cream sauce are sure to please even the pickiest palates.

Softened butter, for the baking dish

1 (15-ounce) container whole-milk ricotta cheese

1 cup freshly grated Parmesan cheese, divided

½ cup chopped frozen spinach, thawed and drained

¼ cup finely chopped roasted red peppers

1 large egg, beaten

¼ teaspoon salt

¼ teaspoon freshly ground black pepper

¼ teaspoon garlic powder

⅔ (12-ounce) box jumbo pasta shells, cooked according to package directions for prebaking (22 to 24 shells)

3 cups heavy cream

1½ cups shredded mozzarella cheese

1. Preheat the oven to 350°F. Butter a 9-by-13-inch baking dish with softened butter.

2. Combine the ricotta cheese, ½ cup of the Parmesan cheese, the spinach, roasted peppers, egg, salt, black pepper, and garlic powder in a large bowl; mix thoroughly.

3. Divide the cheese mixture evenly among the cooked, cooled pasta shells. (Discard any broken shells that are not suitable for stuffing.) Transfer the filled shells to the prepared baking dish.

4. Whisk together the heavy cream and the remaining ½ cup Parmesan cheese in a medium bowl. Pour over the pasta shells. Sprinkle with the mozzarella.

5. Bake for 25 minutes or until the sauce is bubbling and the tops of the shells are golden brown. Let stand for 5 minutes before serving.

CAJUN MAC AND CHEESE

The Cajun contribution in this dish is by way of spicy Andouille sausage and the addition of onions and sweet peppers. With a trifecta of butter, heavy cream, and cheese, the dish is decadent—and absolutely delicious.

- 2 tablespoons butter
- 2 large yellow onions, finely diced (about 2 cups)
- 2 cups finely diced bell peppers (2 cups)
- 1 cup sliced Andouille sausage
- 4 cups heavy cream
- 2 cups shredded Cheddar cheese
- ¼ teaspoon salt
- ½ teaspoon freshly ground black pepper
- 1 pound bow-tie pasta, cooked according to package directions
- ¼ cup sliced green onions

1. Melt the butter in an extra-large skillet over medium-high heat. Add the onions and bell peppers and cook until the vegetables begin to soften, 5 to 6 minutes. Add the sausage and cook for another 5 to 6 minutes or until the vegetables are soft and the sausage begins to brown.

2. Pour in the heavy cream and increase the heat to high. Bring to a boil, then turn the heat to low and simmer until the cream has thickened slightly, about 5 minutes.

3. Add the cheese and stir until melted and combined. Season with salt and black pepper. Add the cooked pasta and stir until all ingredients are well combined and the pasta is coated with sauce.

4. Serve immediately topped with a sprinkling of green onions.

Dairy cattle get excellent veterinary care. It reflects the special relationship between the farmers and their animals, and it makes sense: Healthy cows are more productive for more years. Veterinarians routinely visit herds to keep them in top shape.

**No-Bake Mac and Cheese with
Crispy Crumb Topping,** page 162

NO-BAKE MAC AND CHEESE WITH CRISPY CRUMB TOPPING

This quick casserole (see page 160) has the crispy topping of an oven-baked mac and cheese without any baking time. Saucepan macaroni is simply transferred to a casserole dish, topped with buttery bread crumbs, and broiled until toasty and golden brown.

¾ cup panko bread crumbs

5 tablespoons butter, divided

¼ teaspoon paprika

3 cups uncooked elbow macaroni

½ cup finely chopped onion

3 tablespoons all-purpose flour

3 cups whole milk

½ teaspoon salt

¼ teaspoon freshly ground black pepper

1 teaspoon dry mustard

4 ounces cream cheese, cut into chunks

2 cups shredded American cheese

2 cups shredded Cheddar cheese

1. Preheat the broiler. Melt 2 tablespoons of the butter. Stir together the panko, the melted butter, and the paprika in a small bowl; set aside.

2. Cook the elbow macaroni according to the package directions in a large saucepan; drain and return to the saucepan. Cover and keep warm.

3. Meanwhile, for the cheese sauce, melt the remaining 3 tablespoons butter in a large saucepan over medium heat. Cook the onion in the hot butter until soft, 5 to 6 minutes. Stir in the flour and cook, stirring constantly, for 1 to 2 minutes. Add the milk all at once, stirring constantly. Cook and stir over medium heat until slightly thickened and bubbly, 4 to 5 minutes. Add the salt, pepper, mustard, and cream cheese; whisk until smooth. Remove from the heat. Add the shredded American and Cheddar cheeses in handfuls, whisking constantly until each handful is melted before adding the next one.

4. Immediately pour the cheese sauce over the cooked macaroni and toss gently to coat. Spoon into a 3-quart casserole dish. Quickly sprinkle the panko mixture over the mac and cheese. Broil 6 inches from the heat for 1 to 2 minutes or until golden brown. Let stand for 5 minutes before serving.

"We have an eighteen-month-old daughter, Lucy, and we want her to have the same farm experiences growing up as we had."—Alise Sjostrom, Minnesota dairy farmer

LUCAS & ALISE SJOSTROM BROOTEN, MINNESOTA

Alise Sjostrom is living her dream. "For ten years, I wanted to come back to my home farm and produce cheese using our own milk," she says. "It's exciting to finally get it going."

In the fall of 2012, she and her husband, Lucas, quit their city jobs to join the dairy farm of her parents, Jerry and Linda Jennissen. Once back at Jer-Lindy Farms in central Minnesota, it didn't take long for Alise to put her dream in place: They're selling their home-produced Cheddar cheese and fresh cheese curds, among other products, from a farm-based store. The milk comes from their 180 Brown Swiss and Holstein cows.

Such expansion ventures aren't cheap, so the Sjostroms turned to the Internet to raise the cash they needed through a business investment program. The program provides startup businesses the opportunity to outline their idea and needs so others can make a contribution. "We had set up our contribution period to be thirty days," says Alise. "We actually reached our goal in twenty days, with 499 contributors.

"We love what we're doing," she continues. "We have an eighteen-month-old daughter, Lucy, and we want her to have the same farm experiences we had growing up. At the end of the day now, we can physically see our accomplishments. Sitting at a computer desk job doesn't always give you that feeling."

Alise says the cheese store, which they call the Redhead Creamery because Alise and her three siblings all have red hair, gives the farm a "front door" for customers to see and experience the whole farm. "Our goal is to be as transparent as possible in what we do and how we do it," Alise says. "We want people to feel good about how we produce food. We take care of the land and the cows, and we are good neighbors in this community."

SALSA MAC WITH COLBY JACK

For a simple dish, macaroni and cheese has almost infinite variations. This version is studded with salsa vegetables and baked in a nine-inch pie plate until it's nice and bubbly.

Softened butter, for the baking dish

1 cup uncooked elbow macaroni

1 tablespoon butter

½ small onion, diced

1 tablespoon all-purpose flour

1¼ cups milk

Salt

Freshly ground black pepper

8 ounces Colby Jack cheese, shredded

1 medium tomato, seeded and diced

½ medium green bell pepper, diced

1 jalapeño pepper, seeded and minced (optional)

1. Preheat the oven to 350°F. Butter a 9-inch glass pie plate with softened butter. Cook the macaroni according to the package directions; drain.

2. Melt the butter in a medium saucepan over medium heat. Sauté the diced onion in the hot butter until translucent, 4 to 5 minutes. Stir in the flour. Whisk in the milk all at once. Season to taste with salt and black pepper. Cook and stir until slightly thickened and bubbling, about 3 minutes.

3. Remove from the heat. Add the cheese in small handfuls, stirring after each addition to completely melt the cheese before adding the next one.

Stir in the cooked macaroni, diced tomato,* bell pepper, and, if desired, jalapeño. Stir to coat the macaroni evenly.

4. Transfer to the prepared pie plate. Bake for 25 to 30 minutes or until bubbling. Let stand for 10 minutes. Slice into 6 wedges to serve.

*TIP Try to avoid adding any juices from the tomato. Excess liquid in the cheese sauce can cause it to curdle and get lumpy.

CHEESEBURGER MAC AND CHEESE

Top this homey, family-friendly casserole with crunchy dill pickles and a sprinkle of chopped raw onions right before serving, if you like.

Nonstick cooking spray

1 tablespoon butter

1 small onion, chopped

1 pound lean ground beef

1 cup chopped green bell pepper

2 garlic cloves, minced

½ teaspoon seasoned salt

¼ teaspoon freshly ground black pepper

1 cup whole wheat elbow macaroni, cooked according to the package directions

1 medium tomato, seeded and chopped

1 (8-ounce) can tomato sauce

1 cup shredded Cheddar cheese

1. Preheat the oven to 350°F. Spray an 8-inch baking dish with nonstick cooking spray; set aside.

2. Melt the butter in a large skillet over medium heat. Add the onion and cook until softened, 5 to 6 minutes. Turn the heat to medium-high. Add the ground beef, bell pepper, and garlic and continue to cook until the meat is browned and no longer pink, 5 to 7 minutes. Season the beef mixture with the seasoned salt and pepper.

3. Spoon the cooked macaroni into the prepared baking dish and spread to an even layer. Using a slotted spoon, transfer the ground beef mixture to the dish and spread on the macaroni. Scatter the tomato over the top. Pour the tomato sauce over the beef. Sprinkle with the cheese.

4. Bake for 20 to 25 minutes or until the cheese is melted and the casserole is bubbling. Let the mac and cheese stand for 5 minutes before serving.

KIDS COOK TONIGHT MENU!
Cheeseburger Mac and Cheese
Tossed green salad
Garlic bread sticks
Microwave Chocolate Pie (page 207)

BEET AND BUTTER LETTUCE SALAD WITH SOUR CREAM–MUSTARD DRESSING

To serve this salad family-style, toss everything in a big bowl, as shown. Drizzle with dressing and lightly toss again before serving. For presentation, build each salad individually on salad plates. The beets can be roasted a day or two ahead of time and stored, peeled and diced, in a tightly sealed container.

2 medium beets, scrubbed and trimmed

2/3 cup sour cream

1 tablespoon snipped fresh chives

2 tablespoons red wine vinegar

1 tablespoon sugar

1/4 teaspoon salt

1/2 teaspoon freshly ground black pepper

1 tablespoon coarse-ground Dijon mustard

Milk, as needed

1 head Bibb or butterhead lettuce, cored and torn into bite-size pieces

1/2 cup chopped walnuts, toasted

1. Preheat the oven to 400°F. Wrap the beets tightly in aluminum foil. Bake until tender when pierced with a fork, about 1 hour. Cool to room temperature, then peel and dice; set aside.

2. For dressing whisk together the sour cream, chives, vinegar, sugar, salt, pepper, and mustard in a medium bowl. Whisk in a little milk, if necessary, to achieve the desired consistency. Cover and chill until serving time.

3. When ready to serve, divide the lettuce among four serving plates. Top with the diced beets. Drizzle each salad with the dressing and top with toasted walnuts. Serve immediately.

HOT CHEESY POTATOES

Gregg and Stephanie Knutsen own and operate G&S Dairy in Harrington, Delaware (see page 95). This yummy dish has been a favorite on their family table for years. "Farm men love their meat and potatoes," Stephanie says, "so I'm always looking for quick and simple potato side dishes to serve. This one is very tasty and hearty!"

Softened butter, for the baking dish

3 large unpeeled russet potatoes, scrubbed and thinly sliced

4 tablespoons butter, melted

1 teaspoon salt

¼ teaspoon freshly ground black pepper

¼ teaspoon dried thyme

2 cups shredded Cheddar cheese

1 tablespoon dried parsley

1. Preheat the oven to 425°F. Butter a 9-by-13-inch baking dish with softened butter.

2. Arrange the potato slices in the prepared baking dish. Drizzle with the melted butter and season with salt, pepper, and thyme.

3. Cover the baking dish tightly with aluminum foil. Bake for 45 minutes. Remove the foil and sprinkle with the cheese and parsley. Return the dish to the oven. Bake, uncovered, for 5 to 10 minutes more or until the cheese is melted. Let stand for 5 minutes before serving.

DAIRY HASH BROWNS

Dairy farmer Betty Janke of Hixton, Wisconsin, makes these incredibly creamy hash browns only for special occasions because they are so rich. Needless to say, she says, her family looks forward to those occasions!

Softened butter, for the baking dish

4 tablespoons butter, melted

2 cups sour cream

1 (10.75-ounce) can condensed cream of chicken soup

2 cups shredded Cheddar cheese

1 teaspoon onion powder

¼ teaspoon freshly ground black pepper

1 (30-ounce) package frozen hash browns (cubed or shredded), thawed

1. Preheat the oven to 350°F. Butter a 9-by-13-inch baking dish with softened butter.

2. Combine the melted butter, sour cream, soup, cheese, onion powder, and pepper in a large bowl. Stir until well combined. Add the hash browns and stir to coat thoroughly.

3. Transfer the hash brown mixture to the prepared baking dish. Smooth the top with a spatula. Bake for 1 hour or until the top is browned and the casserole is bubbling. Let the casserole stand for 10 minutes before serving.

Today generations of dairy farm families stand proudly on fields once managed by their ancestors. The industry often spans family histories of a century or more. Dairy farming is as inherent to their makeup as their DNA.

AFTER-DINNER
dessert

FRUIT DESSERTS · CUSTARDS AND PUDDINGS · CREPES
CHEESECAKES · BROWNIES AND BARS · COOKIES · CAKES · PIES

RECITES

BAKED APPLES WITH CINNAMON YOGURT TOPPING

An old-fashioned favorite takes a different form in this warm dessert. The apples are baked in slices rather than whole, then topped with a spoonful of cool, creamy yogurt.

APPLES
Softened butter, for the
  baking dish

4 Granny Smith apples,
  peeled, cored, and sliced

½ cup unsweetened apple
  juice or apple cider

¾ cup light brown sugar

2 tablespoons cornstarch

¼ teaspoon ground cinnamon

¼ teaspoon ground nutmeg

¼ teaspoon salt

CINNAMON YOGURT

1 cup plain Greek yogurt

1 tablespoon honey

½ teaspoon ground cinnamon

1. For the apples, preheat the oven to 350°F. Butter an 8-inch square baking dish with softened butter.

2. Toss the apples with the apple juice in a medium bowl. Mix the brown sugar, cornstarch, cinnamon, nutmeg, and salt in a small bowl. Sprinkle over the apples. Stir gently until the apples are thoroughly coated.

3. Pour the apple mixture into the prepared baking dish. Bake for 40 minutes or until the apples are slightly browned at the edges and the sauce is bubbling.

4. For the cinnamon yogurt, combine the yogurt, honey, and cinnamon in a small bowl.

5. Serve the warm apples topped with the cinnamon yogurt.

HONEY-BAKED PEARS WITH VANILLA YOGURT AND GRANOLA

Bartlett pears have creamy, sweet, and aromatic flesh and are very juicy when ripe. D'Anjou pears—which can be red or green—have a refreshing flavor and slightly firmer flesh than Bartletts. Either variety works beautifully in this simple fruit dessert.

4 medium ripe Bartlett or D'Anjou pears, halved and cored, skins on

½ cup apple juice

1 tablespoon honey

2 cups vanilla Greek yogurt

¾ cup granola

Fresh mint leaves, for garnish

1. Preheat the oven to 400°F. Place the halved pears, cut sides down, in a 2-quart rectangular baking dish.

2. Combine the apple juice and honey in a small saucepan. Cook and stir over low heat until the honey dissolves, 2 to 3 minutes. Pour over the pears. Bake for 35 minutes or until the pears are tender.

3. Divide the yogurt among four shallow bowls. When the pears are done, transfer to a plate and keep warm. Carefully pour the baking liquid into a small saucepan and bring to a boil. Reduce the heat to medium and simmer until reduced to ¼ cup.

4. To serve, place the warm pear halves, cut sides up, on the yogurt in each bowl. Top with the granola and drizzle with the syrup. Top each serving with a mint leaf and serve immediately.

BREAD CUSTARD

Special foods have a way of making and keeping memories. This comforting dessert comes from Betsy Sattazahn of Womelsdorf, Pennsylvania. It was a favorite of her husband, Dennis, as he was growing up. Although his mother, Elsie, passed away before Betsy met Dennis, Elsie's sweet and simple dessert remains beloved by Betsy's family today.

3 tablespoons butter, softened, plus more for the baking dish

¾ cup raisins

5 large eggs

4 cups milk

1 cup granulated sugar

¼ cup all-purpose flour

1 teaspoon vanilla extract

3 slices white sandwich bread

1. Preheat the oven to 400°F. Butter a 2-quart casserole dish; scatter the raisins in the bottom of the prepared dish; set aside.

2. Whisk the eggs and milk in a large mixing bowl. Whisk in the sugar, flour, and vanilla extract. Pour the custard over the raisins in the casserole dish.

3. Cut each slice of bread in half diagonally. Butter both sides of each bread triangle. Arrange the bread pieces on the custard to cover.

4. Fill a large baking dish with 1 inch of warm water. Place the casserole dish in the water bath. Bake for 50 to 55 minutes or until the bread is lightly browned and puffed. Transfer to a wire rack and let cool slightly before serving, about 30 minutes.

Careful control of diet and consumption helps ensure healthy animals and milk production.

PEANUT BUTTER PUDDING PARFAITS

Warm peanut butter–flavored pudding is layered with chocolate chips so the chocolate chips melt and can be swirled through the pudding—too much fun!

⅔ cup sugar

¼ cup cornstarch

3 cups milk

½ cup creamy peanut butter

1 teaspoon vanilla extract

½ cup chocolate chips

1. Combine the sugar and cornstarch in a saucepan. Gradually whisk in the milk. Bring just to a boil over medium heat; reduce the heat and simmer for 2 minutes or until thickened, whisking constantly to avoid burning. Remove from the heat. Whisk in the peanut butter and vanilla extract until the pudding is smooth. Allow to cool slightly, about 5 minutes.

2. To assemble the parfaits, place about ¼ cup of the pudding in each of four parfait glasses or goblets. Sprinkle each with 2 teaspoons of the chocolate chips. Repeat twice with the remaining pudding and chocolate chips to make three layers, ending with chocolate chips. Serve immediately.

Lemon-Berry Crepes, page 182

LEMON-BERRY CREPES

All the steps to make this elegant dessert can be done a day ahead. The crepes, lemon sauce, and cream cheese–yogurt filling can be made and refrigerated. Assembling the desserts is as simple as filling the crepes, drizzling with sauce, and topping with fresh berries. (Recipe pictured on page 180.)

1 tablespoon unsalted butter

1 cup sugar

1 tablespoon lemon zest (from 1 large lemon)

6 tablespoons fresh lemon juice (from 2 lemons)

1 large egg

¼ cup heavy cream

8 ounces strawberry-flavored cream cheese, at room temperature

1 cup plain yogurt

12 Browned Butter Crepes (see page 183)

4 cups assorted fresh berries, such as blueberries, raspberries, and sliced strawberries

1. Melt the butter in a medium saucepan over medium-low heat. Remove from the heat and whisk in the sugar, lemon zest, and lemon juice. Add the egg and whisk until smooth.

2. Return the saucepan to medium-low heat and cook, whisking constantly, until the sauce thickens and coats the back of a spoon, about 5 minutes. (Do not boil or the eggs will scramble.) Remove from the heat. Whisk in the cream and set aside to cool.

3. Beat the cream cheese and yogurt in a medium mixing bowl with an electric mixer on medium-high speed until combined.

4. To serve, spread about 2½ tablespoons of the filling on one half of each crepe. Fold crepe in half over the filling, then fold almost in half again. Place two filled crepes on each serving plate.

5. Top each serving with a generous tablespoon of lemon sauce and some fresh berries. Serve immediately.

ANNIVERSARY DINNER MENU
Pomegranate Spinach Salad (page 98)
Apricot-Dijon Pork Chops with Potato Pancakes
  and Herbed Sour Cream (page 140)
Steamed buttered broccoli
Wild rice
Lemon-Berry Crepes

BROWNED-BUTTER CREPES WITH CITRUS BUTTER AND BLUEBERRY SAUCE

Browned butter gives these crepes deliciously nutty flavor.

CREPES

- 2 tablespoons unsalted butter, plus more for the pan
- 2 large eggs
- 1 cup milk
- ¾ cup all-purpose flour
- 6 tablespoons cornstarch
- ¼ teaspoon salt
- ½ teaspoon vanilla extract

BLUEBERRY SAUCE

- 1½ cups fresh or frozen blueberries
- ¼ cup sugar
- 4 teaspoons fresh lemon juice
- 4 teaspoons cornstarch
- ½ teaspoon vanilla extract
- 2 teaspoons lemon zest

CITRUS BUTTER

- 6 tablespoons unsalted butter, softened
- 2 tablespoons sugar
- 2 teaspoons orange zest
- 2 teaspoons lemon zest
- Pinch of salt

1. For crepe batter, melt the 2 tablespoons butter in a small saucepan over medium heat until light brown. Immediately remove from heat. Skim off solids; set aside.

2. Combine the eggs, milk, and ¼ cup water in a blender and blend on medium speed until smooth. Add the flour, cornstarch, and salt. Add the browned butter and vanilla extract. Blend until smooth. Refrigerate the batter for 30 minutes.

3. Melt a pat of butter in a 6-inch nonstick skillet over medium heat. Pour a scant ¼ cup batter into the skillet, tilting the skillet so the batter covers the bottom in a thin layer. Cook until the crepe is lightly browned, about 1½ minutes. Loosen a corner of the crepe, turn over, and cook until very lightly browned, another 15 seconds. Transfer to a plate. Continue cooking crepes, stacking until there are at least 12, adding more butter to the pan as necessary. Cool to room temperature.

4. Cover the crepes with plastic wrap until ready to use. (Crepes should be refrigerated if stored overnight.)

5. For the blueberry sauce, combine the blueberries, ⅓ cup water, the sugar, and lemon juice in a medium saucepan. Cook over medium heat, stirring frequently, until the sauce comes to a low boil. Mix together the cornstarch and 4 teaspoons cold water in a small bowl. Stir into the blueberry sauce. Simmer until the sauce is thick enough to coat the back of a spoon, 2 to 3 minutes. Remove from the heat and stir in the vanilla extract and lemon zest. Set aside to cool.

6. For the citrus butter, combine the butter, sugar, zests, and salt in a small bowl.

7. To serve, spread about ½ tablespoon of the citrus butter over each crepe. Fold the crepes in quarters and transfer to a serving platter. Top with blueberry sauce.

GUERNSEY

GOLDEN RICHES Known for their yellow-gold color milk and moderate size, Guernsey cows average 1,800 gallons annual milk production. The rich golden color of the milk results from a diet that is high in beta-carotene, earning Guernsey cows the designation "the cheese breed."

STRENGTHS Guernseys are among the most docile of the dairy breeds, as a result of centuries of breeding for that trait. Their milk is high in butterfat, protein, vitamin D, and calcium, which contributes to the fine cheeses consumers enjoy. The cows are natural grazers and do well on all-graze dairies.

ORIGIN First bred in France, then brought to the British isle of Guernsey. They were imported to North America in the 1830s.

"WOW" COW Trotacre Tiller Brenna set a world record for milk production in one year by a Guernsey cow: 5,500 gallons. She lives at Trotacre Farms of Enon Valley, Pennsylvania.

"Brenna is very sound on her feet and legs and has a lot of width," says Dave Trotter in his best cattle judging terms. "She is also very aggressive at the feed bunk, where she shares space with 170 other cows." What Dave likes best about her is that she is home-bred from one of their family-owned sires, an accomplished World Dairy Expo Premier Sire for several years. While Dave loves the Guernseys, he has other breeds in his herd, including Holstein, Ayrshire, and Jersey cows. "I chose to diversify so that all of my daughters—Abby, Bethany, Cara, and Jamie—had some individuality when showing at the fair," he says in emphasis of the family nature of his dairy farm.

BOURBON SWEET POTATO CHEESECAKE

For sweet potato purée, bake two large sweet potatoes in a 400°F oven for forty-five to fifty-five minutes or until tender. When cool, scoop the flesh into a bowl. Purée in a food processor or food mill.

CRUST
Softened butter, for the pan

2   cups finely ground gingersnap cookies

6   tablespoons butter, melted

FILLING

3   (8-ounce) packages cream cheese, at room temperature

½   cup (1 stick) unsalted butter, at room temperature

1   cup sugar

2   cups sweet potato purée

3   tablespoons bourbon or apple cider

1   teaspoon ground ginger

1   teaspoon ground cinnamon

¾   teaspoon ground nutmeg

2   tablespoons heavy cream

4   large eggs, at room temperature

TOPPING

1½ cups sour cream

2   tablespoons sugar

1½ tablespoons bourbon

1. Preheat the oven to 350°F. Place the oven rack in the lower third of the oven. Generously butter a 10-inch springform pan; set aside.

2. For the crust, combine the cookie crumbs and melted butter in a medium bowl. Press the crumbs evenly on the bottom and ½ inch up the sides of the prepared pan. Bake for about 8 minutes or until the edges of the crust are lightly browned. Cool on a wire rack.

3. For the filling, combine the cream cheese, butter, and sugar in a large mixing bowl. Beat with an electric mixer on medium speed until combined, scraping the bowl as necessary. Add the sweet potato purée and mix until blended. Beat in the bourbon, ginger, cinnamon, nutmeg, and the heavy cream. Add the eggs, two at a time, beating after each addition. Mix until the eggs are incorporated and the batter is smooth.

4. Pour the batter into the crust. Bake for 20 minutes. Reduce the oven temperature to 325°F and bake for 20 minutes. Reduce the oven temperature to 300°F and bake for 20 minutes. Reduce the temperature to 225°F and bake just until the cake is set around the edge but still slightly jiggly in the center, 15 to 20 minutes.

5. Meanwhile, for the topping, whisk together the sour cream, sugar, and bourbon in a small bowl.

6. Transfer the cheesecake to a rack. Turn the oven to 350°F. Spread the topping evenly over the cheesecake. Bake just until the topping is set, 5 minutes. Remove cheesecake from the oven and carefully run a paring knife around the edge of the cake. Cool completely on a wire rack. Cover and refrigerate the cooled cheesecake for several hours or up to two days. Remove springform ring before serving.

K'S SUNDAY CHEESECAKE

This simple cheesecake, made in a nine-inch baking pan, comes from Karen Valenti of Kansas City. It can be whipped up in just a few minutes on days when you have a long to-do list—or when you would like to spend time doing things other than baking. Flavored with vanilla and almond extract, it is lovely plain or adorned with fresh berries. Karen grew up on a farm in Kansas, and her daughter, Samantha Carter, works for the Midwest Dairy Association. "I love hearing about her job and adventures," Karen says, because it makes her think of her childhood on the farm. "Always great memories!"

CRUST
Softened butter, for the pan
¾ cup graham cracker crumbs
½ cup sugar
4 tablespoons unsalted
  butter, melted

FILLING
2 large eggs
2 (8-ounce) packages cream
  cheese, softened
1 cup sugar
1 teaspoon vanilla extract
¼ teaspoon almond extract
Fresh strawberries,
  raspberries, blackberries,
  and/or blueberries
  (optional)

1. Preheat the oven to 300°F. Butter the bottom and sides of a 9-inch baking pan. Set the pan aside.

2. For the crust, combine the graham cracker crumbs, sugar, and melted butter in a medium bowl and mix thoroughly. Transfer the crumb mixture to the prepared pan and press evenly on the bottom and slightly up the sides of the pan to make a crust.

3. For the cake, combine the eggs and cream cheese in a medium mixing bowl and beat with an electric mixer on medium speed until smooth. Add the sugar, vanilla extract, and almond extract; mix until well blended. Pour the filling over the crust.

4. Bake for 45 to 50 minutes or until the middle is set, with just a slight jiggle. Cool completely on a wire rack. Cover and chill for at least 4 hours before serving. Top with fresh berries, if desired.

PENNSYLVANIA DUTCH BLUEBERRY TORTE

This cream cheese–filled blueberry dessert comes from Raechel Kilgore Sattazahn of Womelsdorf, Pennsylvania. It's been a favorite of the Kilgore family of Airville, Pennsylvania, for generations. This version calls for homemade blueberry topping, but if you're pressed for time, do as Raechel's family does and substitute a can of blueberry pie filling.

CRUST
Softened butter, for the pan

1 cup all-purpose flour

¼ cup powdered sugar

1 tablespoon cornstarch

¼ teaspoon salt

⅓ cup cold unsalted butter, cut into chunks

BLUEBERRY TOPPING

6 cups fresh blueberries

¼ cup granulated sugar

1 tablespoon plus 1½ teaspoons cornstarch

1 teaspoon ground cinnamon

2 tablespoons cold unsalted butter, cut into chunks

1 tablespoon fresh lemon juice

CREAM CHEESE FILLING

1 (8-ounce) package cream cheese, softened

1 cup powdered sugar

2 cups heavy cream

1. For the crust, preheat the oven to 350°F. Butter a 9-inch square baking pan with the softened butter; set aside.

2. Combine the flour, powdered sugar, cornstarch, and salt in a medium bowl. Use a pastry blender to cut in the cold butter until the mixture resembles coarse crumbs. Press into the bottom of the prepared pan. Bake for 18 to 20 minutes or until the edges are light brown. Allow to cool completely on a wire rack.

3. For the blueberry topping, combine the blueberries, granulated sugar, cornstarch, cinnamon, and ¾ cup water in a large saucepan over medium-low heat. Cook and stir until the sugar is dissolved, the mixture thickens slightly, and the berries start to break down, 20 to 25 minutes. Remove from the heat and stir in the butter and lemon juice. Allow to cool completely; set aside.

4. For the cream cheese filling, beat the cream cheese and powdered sugar with an electric mixer until smooth and creamy. Add the heavy cream and beat until smooth.

5. Spread the filling evenly in the cooled crust, spreading it to edges. Top with the blueberry topping, spreading it to the edges. Cover and chill for at least 4 hours or overnight before serving.

BUTTERMILK BROWNIES

The buttermilk in these cakelike brownies makes them unbelievably moist, while the buttermilk in the frosting gives it a delightful tang.

BROWNIES
Softened butter, for the pan

½ cup (1 stick) unsalted butter

¼ cup unsweetened cocoa powder

½ cup vegetable oil

2 cups all-purpose flour

1 teaspoon baking soda

½ teaspoon salt

2 cups granulated sugar

2 large eggs

¼ cup buttermilk

¼ teaspoon vanilla extract

FROSTING

½ cup (1 stick) unsalted butter

½ cup buttermilk

¼ cup unsweetened cocoa powder

1 (1-pound) box powdered sugar (4¾ cups)

1 teaspoon vanilla extract

Pinch of salt

1. For the brownies, preheat the oven to 400°F. Butter a 9 by 13-inch baking pan with softened butter; set the pan aside.

2. Heat the butter, cocoa powder, vegetable oil, and 1 cup water in a medium saucepan over medium-high heat. Bring to a boil. Remove from the heat and allow to cool just until warm; set aside.

2. Sift the flour, baking soda, and salt into a medium bowl; set aside.

3. Combine the granulated sugar, eggs, buttermilk, and vanilla extract in a large bowl. Whisk to combine. Add the cooled cocoa mixture.

4. Add the dry ingredients to the wet ingredients and stir just until combined. Pour the batter into the prepared baking pan. Bake for about 20 minutes or until a cake tester inserted into the center comes out clean.

5. For the frosting, combine the butter, buttermilk, and cocoa powder in a saucepan. Bring to a boil over medium-high heat. Remove from the heat.

6. Combine the powdered sugar, vanilla extract, and salt in a large mixing bowl. Slowly add the buttermilk mixture to the sugar mixture, beating with an electric mixer on medium speed. Continue beating until smooth and creamy. Allow to cool completely.

7. After the brownies have cooled, spread the frosting evenly over the top.

PUMPKIN PIE SQUARES WITH CINNAMON-SUGAR YOGURT TOPPING

The graham cracker–oat crust, classic pumpkin pie filling, and topping of crunchy toasted pecans and creamy cinnamon-flavored yogurt make this dessert from the Anglin family of Bentonville, Arkansas, perfect for a fall potluck. Fourth-generation dairy farmers Ryan and Susan Anglin—together with their sons, Cody and Casey—run Triple A Farms, which has grown from seventeen cows in 1972 to 300 today.

CRUST
Softened butter, for the baking dish
1 cup graham cracker crumbs
½ cup old-fashioned oats
¼ cup light brown sugar
4 tablespoons butter, melted
2 tablespoons milk

FILLING
1 (15-ounce) can pumpkin purée
2 large eggs, beaten
¾ cup granulated sugar
¾ cup vanilla yogurt
½ cup milk
1 teaspoon ground cinnamon
1 teaspoon pumpkin pie spice
¼ teaspoon salt
½ cup chopped pecans

TOPPING
1 cup plain Greek yogurt
2 teaspoons granulated sugar
1 teaspoon ground cinnamon

1. For the crust, preheat the oven to 350°F. Butter a 9 by 13-inch baking dish with the softened butter; set aside.

2. For the crust, combine the graham cracker crumbs, oats, brown sugar, melted butter, and milk in a medium bowl. Press the mixture evenly into the bottom of the prepared baking dish. Bake for 10 minutes or until lightly golden brown.

3. For the filling, combine the pumpkin, eggs, granulated sugar, yogurt, milk, cinnamon, pumpkin pie spice, and salt; mix until thoroughly blended. Pour the filling into the baked crust and spread evenly. Bake for 30 minutes or until the filling is almost set.

4. Sprinkle the pecans evenly over the filling and bake for 10 to 15 minutes more or until the center is set. Transfer the dish to a wire rack to cool completely.

5. For the topping, mix the yogurt, granulated sugar, and cinnamon in a small bowl; cover and chill until ready to serve.

6. To serve, cut into squares. Top each square with a dollop of yogurt topping.

PISTACHIO-DRIED CHERRY BISCOTTI WITH WHITE CHOCOLATE DRIZZLE

With bright green pistachios and dark red dried cherries, these crunchy Italian-style cookies make an eye-catching and festive Christmas treat—they taste delicious, too!

COOKIES

Softened butter, for the baking sheet

- 4 tablespoons unsalted butter, softened
- ⅔ cup sugar
- 2 large eggs
- 1 teaspoon vanilla extract
- 2 cups all-purpose flour
- 1½ teaspoons baking powder
- ¼ teaspoon salt
- ⅔ cup shelled pistachios
- ⅔ cup dried cherries

DRIZZLE

- 4 ounces white chocolate, finely chopped
- ½ teaspoon unsalted butter

1. For the cookies, preheat the oven to 350°F. Butter a nonstick baking sheet with softened butter.

2. Beat together the butter and sugar in a large mixing bowl with an electric mixer on medium speed until light and fluffy, 1 to 2 minutes. Add the eggs and vanilla extract and beat until combined, scraping the bowl as necessary.

3. Sift together the flour, baking powder, and salt. Gradually add the dry ingredients to the egg mixture, beating until combined. With a spoon, stir in the pistachios and cherries and mix until evenly distributed. (The dough will be fairly soft and sticky.)

5. Turn the dough out onto a lightly floured surface and divide in half. Roll each portion into a 12-by-1¼-inch log. Place the logs, 3 inches apart, on the prepared baking sheet and flatten the tops slightly. Bake for 30 to 35 minutes or until lightly browned. Transfer the baking sheet to a wire rack and allow to cool for 10 minutes. Lower the oven temperature to 300°F.

6. Using a serrated knife, cut the biscotti at a 45-degree angle into ¾-inch slices. Arrange the slices on the baking sheet. (Butter a second baking sheet and divide the cookies between the two, if necessary.)

7. Bake the cookies for another 15 minutes or until the edges start to brown, turning them halfway through the baking time. Remove from the oven and cool on a wire rack.

8. For the drizzle, microwave the white chocolate and butter in a small microwave-safe bowl on 50% (medium) power until melted. Drizzle the chocolate over the cooled biscotti.

ESPRESSO SHORTBREAD SANDWICH COOKIES

Bittersweet chocolate ganache is sandwiched between two rich, tender, coffee-flavored shortbread cookies. The flavors of chocolate and coffee go together like hand in glove.

COOKIES

1	cup (2 sticks) unsalted butter, softened
½	cup sugar
2½	cups all-purpose flour
6	tablespoons instant espresso powder
⅛	teaspoon salt

FILLING

½	cup heavy cream
4	ounces bittersweet chocolate, chopped

1. For the cookies, combine the butter, sugar, flour, espresso powder, and salt in a large mixing bowl. Mix with an electric mixer on low speed just until the dough comes together. Wrap the dough in plastic wrap and chill for 1 hour.

2. Preheat the oven to 350°F. Transfer the dough to a lightly floured surface and roll to ¼-inch thickness. Using a 2-inch round cookie cutter, cut out the cookies and place them 2 inches apart on a nonstick baking sheet. (You should have about 32 cookies.)

3. Bake for about 10 minutes or until the cookies are firm. Transfer the baking sheet to a wire rack and cool completely, about 30 minutes.

4. For the filling, bring the cream to a boil in a saucepan over medium heat. Remove from the heat and add the chocolate. Whisk until smooth. Allow to cool until the filling is spreadable consistency, about 30 minutes.

5. To assemble sandwich cookies, spread each of the bottoms of half the cookies with 2 teaspoons of the chocolate filling. Top with the remaining cookies, bottom sides together. Let stand for 2 to 3 hours to allow the chocolate to set up.

CORNMEAL RASPBERRY LINZER COOKIES

Cornmeal adds pleasing crunch to this buttery sandwich cookie version of linzertorte, the famous Austrian dessert. A linzer cookie cutter set makes cutting the cookies a snap.

¾ cup (1½ sticks) unsalted butter, softened
¾ cup granulated sugar
1 large egg
1½ cups all-purpose flour
½ cup yellow cornmeal
½ teaspoon salt
½ cup seedless raspberry jam
 Powdered sugar, for dusting

1. Combine the butter and granulated sugar in a large mixing bowl. Beat with an electric mixer on medium-high speed until light and fluffy, scraping down the sides of the bowl as necessary. Add the egg and beat until combined. Add the flour, cornmeal, and salt and mix thoroughly on low speed, scraping down the sides of the bowl several times if necessary.

2. Divide the dough in half. Pat each portion into a flattened round. Wrap each round in plastic wrap and chill in the refrigerator for 1 hour or until easy to handle.

3. Preheat the oven to 375°F. Remove one portion of the dough from the refrigerator and let it stand for 5 minutes. Roll out the dough on a lightly floured surface to ⅛- to ¼-inch thickness. Using a

2½-inch cookie cutter, cut the dough into the desired shapes. Place the cutouts 1 inch apart on a large nonstick cookie sheet. Using a ¾-inch cookie cutter, cut shapes from centers of half the cookies. Reroll the scraps as necessary. Repeat with the remaining portion of dough. Bake in batches, if necessary.

4. Bake for 7 to 10 minutes or until the edges are light brown. Transfer the cookies to a wire rack to cool.

5. To assemble the cookies, spread a scant teaspoon of the raspberry jam on each cookie bottom (without cutouts). Top with the cookies with cutout centers. Serve within 2 hours. Right before serving, dust with powdered sugar.

Pear Vanilla Cream Cake with Chocolate Glaze, page 200

PEAR VANILLA CREAM CAKE WITH CHOCOLATE GLAZE

Save making this dessert for a special occasion, when you can invest the time it takes. Beautiful, elegant, and very impressive, it requires true commitment—which will be greatly rewarded! (See page 198.)

PASTRY CREAM

- 2 large egg yolks
- 2 tablespoons sugar
- 4½ teaspoons cornstarch
- ½ cup plus 2 tablespoons milk
- ½ teaspoon vanilla extract
- 1 tablespoon unsalted butter

CHOCOLATE GLAZE

- ½ cup heavy cream
- 2 teaspoons light corn syrup
- 4 teaspoons unsalted butter
- 4 ounces bittersweet chocolate, finely chopped

PEARS

- 2 ripe Bosc pears, peeled, cored, and sliced ¼ inch thick
- 4 teaspoons sugar
- 1½ teaspoons fresh lemon juice

CAKE

Softened butter, for the baking pans

All-purpose flour, for the baking pans

- 1½ cups all-purpose flour
- 2 teaspoons baking powder
- ¼ teaspoon salt
- 4 tablespoons unsalted butter

- 1 cup sugar
- ½ cup milk
- 1 teaspoon vanilla extract
- 2 large eggs

1. For the pastry cream, whisk together the egg yolks and sugar in a small bowl until smooth. Whisk in the cornstarch.

2. Heat the milk and vanilla extract in a saucepan over medium heat; bring to a low boil. Very slowly whisk the hot milk into the egg mixture. Pour the liquid back into the saucepan and cook over medium-low heat, stirring constantly, until it thickens, about 3 minutes.

3. Remove the saucepan from the heat and whisk in the butter. Transfer the pastry cream to a clean bowl. Place plastic wrap directly on the surface of the pastry cream to prevent a skin from forming. Refrigerate until cold, 2 to 3 hours.

4. For the chocolate glaze, heat the cream, corn syrup, and butter in a saucepan over medium heat until it bubbles, about 3 minutes. Remove the pan from the heat and add the chocolate. Whisk until smooth. Place the pan on a wire rack and cool until the glaze has thickened slightly but remains pourable, about 15 minutes. (Note: The glaze can be reheated if it gets too thick. To reheat, place over low heat, stirring constantly, until pourable consistency.)

5. For the pears, combine the pears, sugar, and lemon juice in a skillet. Cook over medium-high heat until the sugar starts to brown slightly but the pears retain their shape, about 10 minutes. As the pears begin to turn light golden brown, stir them gently to prevent burning. Remove from the heat and allow to cool.

6. For the cake, preheat the oven to 350°F. Butter and flour two 9-inch round cake pans. Sift together the flour, baking powder, and salt. Set aside. Beat together the butter and sugar in a large mixing bowl with an electric mixer on medium-high speed until light and fluffy, about 3 minutes.

7. Combine the milk and vanilla extract in a small bowl. Alternately add the dry ingredients and the milk mixture to the creamed butter in three additions. Beat on medium speed until smooth. Add the eggs, one at a time, beating well after each addition.

8. Divide the cake batter between the prepared pans. Bake for 20 to 25 minutes or until a cake tester inserted in the center of the cake layers comes out clean. Cool the layers on wire racks for 10 minutes. Remove the layers from the pans and cool completely on wire racks.

9. To assemble the cake, place one layer on a cake plate. Spread the pastry cream evenly over the cake layer. Carefully arrange the pears on the pastry cream. Top with the remaining cake layer. Before serving, pour and spread the chocolate glaze over the top of the cake, allowing it to drip down the sides of the cake.

TRIPLE-LAYER CHOCOLATE CAKE WITH VANILLA BUTTERCREAM

Karen Bohnert of East Moline, Illinois, remembers her late mother, Michelle, making this indulgent cake for Easter dinner, family picnics, and "where other dairy farm families would gather." Now Karen makes this cake in honor of her mother. "We salute Grandma Michelle with this cake," she says, "and raise a glass of milk."

CAKE
Softened butter, for the baking pans
- 1 cup unsweetened cocoa powder
- ½ cup (1 stick) unsalted butter, softened
- 1¾ cups granulated sugar
- 3 large eggs, at room temperature
- 1½ teaspoons vanilla extract
- 2¼ cups all-purpose flour
- 2 teaspoons baking powder
- ½ teaspoon baking soda
- ½ teaspoon salt

FILLING
- 2 cups powdered sugar
- 4 tablespoons unsalted butter, softened
- 2 tablespoons vanilla extract

FROSTING
- ¾ cup chocolate chips
- ½ cup heavy cream
- 4 tablespoons butter
- 2½ cups powdered sugar

1. For the cake, preheat the oven to 350°F. Butter three 9-inch round nonstick cake pans and line the bottoms with waxed paper.

2. Bring 2 cups of water to a boil in a medium saucepan over medium-high heat. Remove from the heat, add the cocoa powder, and whisk until smooth. Allow to cool to room temperature, about 30 minutes.

3. Beat the butter in a large mixing bowl with an electric mixer on medium speed for 1 minute. Add the granulated sugar and beat until fluffy, about 2 minutes, scraping down the sides of the bowl occasionally. Add the eggs and vanilla extract and beat until well blended.

4. In a separate bowl, whisk together the flour, baking powder, baking soda, and salt. Alternately add the dry ingredients and the cooled cocoa mixture to the butter mixture in three additions. Beat until thoroughly mixed.

5. Divide the batter evenly among the prepared pans. Bake for 25 to 30 minutes or until a cake tester inserted in the centers of the cakes comes out clean. Transfer the pans to wire racks. Let cool in the pans for 10 minutes. Remove the cake layers from the pans and gently peel off the waxed paper. Let cool completely.

6. For the filling, beat together the powdered sugar, butter, and vanilla extract until smooth and spreadable. Set aside.

continued on page 204

continued from page 202

7. For the frosting, combine the chocolate chips, heavy cream, and butter in a medium saucepan over medium-low heat, whisking until melted. Gradually add the powdered sugar and whisk thoroughly. Remove the pan from the heat and place in a large bowl that is partially filled with ice to cool, 5 to 10 minutes. Stir occasionally while cooling to prevent the frosting from becoming too stiff.

8. To assemble the cake, place a layer on a serving plate. (Use a serrated knife to trim the cake layers to a level surface if necessary.) Spread with half the filling. Add the second layer and spread with the remaining filling. Top with the third cake layer. Spread the cooled frosting on the top and sides of the cake.

9. Serve immediately or cover the cake with a large bowl or a cake keeper and refrigerate up to 3 days. Let the cake stand at room temperature for 30 minutes before serving.

Dairy herds adapt to many environments, from mountain slopes to the arid Southwest. Dairy farmers can offset heat with shade, fans, and misting systems to keep their animals comfortable.

COCOA-BERRY YOGURT TARTS

When you need a fun, fresh, pretty dessert really fast, look to these individual ricotta-filled and berry-topped tarts. It takes just fifteen minutes or less to put them together!

1   cup vanilla yogurt

1   cup whole-milk ricotta cheese

2   tablespoons sugar

2   tablespoons unsweetened cocoa powder

6   mini graham cracker pie crusts

1   cup fresh raspberries, blueberries, or sliced strawberries

1. Whisk the yogurt, ricotta, sugar, and cocoa powder in a large bowl until thoroughly combined and creamy. Divide the mixture among the six pie crusts. Top with the fresh berries. Serve immediately.

The process of milking has come a long way from a rudimentary bucket and milking stool. Modern milking machinery ensures efficiency, comfort, and a safe product.

CHOCOLATE–GRAND MARNIER FUDGE PIE

This decadent, intensely chocolate, adults-only pie packs a wallop of orange flavor from a generous dose of Grand Marnier.

1   **(9-inch) frozen deep-dish pie shell**

4   **ounces unsweetened chocolate, coarsely chopped**

10 **tablespoons unsalted butter, cut into large chunks**

2   **large eggs**

2   **large egg yolks**

1   **cup granulated sugar**

½   **cup all-purpose flour**

1   **teaspoon salt**

1   **teaspoon vanilla extract**

½   **cup Grand Marnier orange liqueur**

2   **tablespoons orange marmalade**

    Powdered sugar

    Whipped cream

1. Preheat the oven to 375°F. Thaw the frozen pie shell at room temperature for 15 minutes. Prick the pastry several times with a fork. Bake just until the surface looks slightly dry, 6 to 7 minutes. Transfer to a wire rack. Turn the oven to 425°F.

2. Microwave the chocolate and butter in a microwave-safe bowl on high in 30-second intervals, stirring after each one, until completely melted. Allow to cool just until slightly warm.

3. Whisk together the eggs, egg yolks, granulated sugar, flour, salt, and vanilla extract in a large mixing bowl. Add the Grand Marnier, marmalade, and chocolate mixture. Whisk until thoroughly blended. Pour the filling into the pie shell.

4. Bake until puffed, set, and slightly crusty on top, 22 to 27 minutes. Transfer to a wire rack and cool completely. To serve, dust with powdered sugar. Top each slice with a spoonful of whipped cream.

MICROWAVE CHOCOLATE PIE

This rich, chocolaty pie is simple to make, and the results will wow even the most refined palate. For a butterscotch variation, eliminate the cocoa power, substitute 1 cup brown sugar for the white sugar, and increase the vanilla to 1 teaspoon.

1 cup sugar

2 tablespoons all-purpose flour

2 tablespoons cornstarch

2 tablespoons unsweetened cocoa powder

Pinch of salt

3 large egg yolks

2 cups milk

1 tablespoon butter, melted

½ teaspoon vanilla extract

1 (9-inch) frozen deep-dish pie shell, baked according to package directions

Whipped cream

1. Combine the sugar, flour, cornstarch, cocoa powder, and salt in a large microwave-safe bowl. Whisk in the egg yolks and milk. Cook for 6 minutes on high. Remove from the microwave and whisk until completely smooth.

2. Whisk in the melted butter and vanilla extract, then pour the filling into the cooled pie shell. Cover the surface with waxed paper to prevent a skin from forming. Refrigerate until cold and firm, at least 2 hours. To serve, cut the pie into wedges and top with a dollop of whipped cream.

However briefly, photographers can be even more interesting than breakfast for a group of curious cows. Apparently there's at least one who isn't so easily distracted from her food.

Honey-Roasted Peanut Caramel Pie, page 211

"Some of our friends don't understand why you can't just take off for the weekend or a holiday. It doesn't work that way on a dairy farm." —Brad Scott, California dairy farmer

BRAD & SALLY SCOTT MORENO VALLEY, CALIFORNIA

It's not easy to farm in Southern California, where urban demands on natural resources are influential. But Scott Brothers Dairy near Moreno Valley has found a way to make it work—and thrive.

"We're less than two hours east of downtown Los Angeles," says Brad Scott, who runs the 1,100-cow Holstein herd with his father, Stan, and brother, Bruce. "We have lots of development all around us."

One way the Scotts work with their community is through a partnership with a nearby municipality to use treated wastewater for crop irrigation. "We have about 900 acres, and 700 of them are irrigated," says Brad. "We also irrigate using wastewater from the dairy and collected rainwater. As a result, we can irrigate with recycled water only." The farm also gets electrical power from solar panels on the roof of its feed storage shed. "We get over 342 days of sunlight a year in this area," Brad says.

While urban pressures make dairy farming difficult here, Brad says the year-round mild temperatures are a mitigating factor. The farm grows seventy percent of the food that the herd needs. "The rest, along with grain, is trucked in," he says.

The century-old farm started by Brad's great-grandfather has its own milk-processing plant in nearby Chino. It's one of the largest manufacturers of frozen yogurt in the world.

"I'm very proud of our farm history," says Brad. "I was born into the dairy business; it's in my blood. There are lots of challenges, but I love the tie to the animals and the land. Some of our friends don't understand why you can't just take off for the weekend or a holiday. It doesn't work that way on a dairy farm."

HONEY-ROASTED PEANUT CARAMEL PIE

Each bite of this sweet-salty pie is like a piece of caramel-nut candy wrapped in pastry. It's absolutely irresistible and guaranteed to satisfy a sweet tooth. (Recipe pictured on page 208.)

- 1 (9-inch) frozen deep-dish pie shell
- ½ cup (1 stick) butter
- ¾ cup light brown sugar
- 2 tablespoons granulated sugar
- 2 tablespoons honey
- ¼ cup heavy cream
- 3 cups lightly salted honey-roasted peanuts

1. Preheat the oven to 400°F. Let the pie shell thaw at room temperature for 10 minutes. Prick with a fork. Bake for 5 minutes or just until the surface looks dry. Cool on a wire rack. Turn the oven temperature to 350°F.

2. Combine the butter, brown sugar, granulated sugar, and honey in a medium saucepan and bring to a simmer over medium heat. Allow to simmer until the mixture reaches 240° to 245°F on a candy thermometer, just above the soft ball stage,* about 4 minutes. Remove the pan from the heat and stir in the heavy cream and the peanuts.

3. Transfer the filling to the partially baked pie shell, making sure to spread nuts in an even layer. Place the pie on a baking sheet and bake for 15 minutes or until the filling is bubbling evenly. Cool completely on a wire rack before serving.

*TIP The soft ball stage is between 234° to 240°F on a candy thermometer. You can also do the water test: Drop a tiny bit of the caramel in ice water. It should form a ball that flattens immediately when pressed.

MACADAMIA ICE CREAM PIE

This chocolate-crusted ice cream pie, studded with toasted coconut and chopped macadamia nuts, is a refreshing make-ahead dessert for a warm summer night.

½ gallon vanilla ice cream

⅔ cup raw macadamia nuts, toasted and chopped (2 ounces)

1 cup shredded coconut, toasted and cooled

1 (9-inch) prepared chocolate cookie pie crust

Whipped cream

Chocolate syrup

Toasted shredded coconut

1. Place the ice cream in a large bowl and stir with a large spoon until softened. Stir the nuts and coconut into the softened ice cream until evenly distributed. Transfer the ice cream mixture to the chocolate cookie crust and cover tightly with plastic wrap. Freeze until firm, 5 hours or overnight.

2. Let the pie stand at room temperature for 10 minutes before serving. Cut the pie into wedges. Top each wedge with whipped cream, a drizzle of chocolate syrup, and toasted coconut.

Rotary milking parlors, or carousels, speed up the milking process for both the farmer and the cows. The carousel moves very slowly, allowing the cows to step on and off the platform safely. It generally takes between seven and nine minutes to milk a single cow.

OLD-FASHIONED SUGAR CREAM PIE

Creamy and scented with vanilla, this nostalgic pie is the essence of simplicity. Mary Lou Topp of Botkins, Ohio, makes her mother's recipe for family and neighborhood get-togethers and gives them away as gifts—especially at Christmas.

1   tablespoon packed light brown sugar

1   tablespoon plus ⅓ cup all-purpose flour, divided

1   (9-inch) frozen deep-dish pie shell, thawed

2   cups heavy cream

1   cup sugar

½   teaspoon vanilla extract

2   tablespoons unsalted butter, cut up

   Ground cinnamon

1. Preheat the oven to 350°F. Whisk together the brown sugar and 1 tablespoon flour in a small bowl. Sprinkle evenly on the bottom of the pie shell.

2. Whisk the cream, sugar, the remaining ⅓ cup flour, and the vanilla extract in a medium mixing bowl until smooth.

3. Place the pie shell on a rimmed baking sheet. Pour the filling into the pie shell (it will be very full). Dot the filling with the butter. Sprinkle with cinnamon. To prevent overbrowning, cover the edge of the pie with aluminum foil.

4. Bake for 40 minutes; remove the foil. Bake for 25 minutes or until the top is lightly browned and the filling is bubbling across the surface. (The pie won't appear set but will firm up upon cooling). Cool the pie completely on a wire rack.

5. Cover and chill for at least 2 hours or up to 24 hours before serving.

FAMILY GATHERINGS
and special occasions

APPETIZERS · BRUNCH · ENTRÉES
SIDES · SPECIAL SWEETS

RECICPES

CHEDDAR AND MUSHROOM BREAKFAST SQUARES

This quick-to-fix strata is the perfect make-ahead breakfast or brunch dish for a small group. Create your own variations with different types of cheese, various vegetables—such as asparagus, spinach, and broccoli florets—or other ingredients such as diced ham or crumbled crisp-cooked bacon.

Softened butter, for the baking dish

2 tablespoons butter

2 cups sliced white button mushrooms

½ cup sliced green onions, white and green parts

6 slices country-style bread, cubed

2 cups shredded Cheddar cheese, divided

2 cups milk

8 large eggs

1 teaspoon red or green hot pepper sauce

¼ teaspoon salt (optional)

1. Butter a 9-inch square glass or ceramic baking dish; set aside.

2. Melt the butter in a medium skillet over medium heat. Add the mushrooms and cook for about 5 minutes or until softened and browned at the edges. Stir in the green onions; set aside.

3. Place half the bread cubes in the prepared baking dish. Scatter half the mushroom mixture and half the cheese over the bread cubes. Layer the remaining bread cubes and mushroom mixture in the dish; set aside.

4. Beat the milk, eggs, hot pepper sauce, and salt, if using, in a large bowl until well blended. Pour over the bread cubes in the baking dish and top with the remaining cheese. Cover the dish with aluminum foil and refrigerate for 8 to 10 hours.

5. Preheat the oven to 350°F. (Allow dish to sit at room temperature while oven is heating.) Bake the casserole, covered, for 45 minutes. Remove the foil and bake for another 15 minutes or until the top is puffed and the cheese is browned at the edges. Let stand for 5 minutes before serving; cut into squares.

SCRAMBLED EGG AND MOZZARELLA PIZZAS

Here's a way to have pizza for breakfast! Kids love these mini pizzas topped with scrambled eggs, cheese, and veggies. Serve two halves as a main course or in singles as part of a brunch buffet.

Nonstick cooking spray

3 cups sliced mushrooms

1½ cups diced red bell pepper

¾ cup sliced green onions, white and green parts (about 6)

12 large eggs

½ teaspoon salt

1 teaspoon freshly ground black pepper

1 teaspoon dried oregano, crushed

½ cup pizza sauce

6 English muffins, split and lightly toasted

3 cups shredded mozzarella cheese

1. Preheat the oven to 350°F. Spray a large nonstick skillet with nonstick cooking spray. Cook and stir the mushrooms, bell pepper, and green onions over medium-high heat until softened, 4 to 5 minutes.

2. Whisk the eggs, salt, black pepper, and oregano in a large bowl. Pour into the skillet and cook over medium-low heat, stirring frequently, until the eggs are cooked through but still creamy, about 5 minutes.

3. Spread 2 teaspoons of the pizza sauce over each English muffin half and place on two large rimmed baking sheets. Divide the scrambled egg mixture among the muffins. Top each with ¼ cup of the cheese.

4. Bake until the cheese is melted, about 5 minutes. Serve immediately.

BROWNED-BUTTER ORANGE AND CRANBERRY CRUMB CAKE

Flavored with cranberries, cinnamon, and orange, this rich coffee cake is ideal for a Christmas brunch. For those who like a buttery streusel topping as much (or more) as the cake, it doesn't get much better than this.

TOPPING

10	tablespoons unsalted butter
1⅓	cups all-purpose flour
¾	cup packed light brown sugar
1	teaspoon ground cinnamon
¼	teaspoon salt

CAKE

Softened butter, for the baking pan

1½	cups all-purpose flour, plus additional for the pan
½	cup plus 2 tablespoons granulated sugar
1½	teaspoons baking powder
½	teaspoon salt
¼	teaspoon ground cinnamon
	Zest of 2 oranges
2	tablespoons unsalted butter
1	large egg
½	cup milk
2	tablespoons orange juice
1¼	teaspoons vanilla extract
1½	cups fresh or frozen cranberries, thawed

1. For the topping, cook and stir the 10 tablespoons butter in a skillet over medium heat until the butter foams, begins to turn light brown, and smells nutty. Remove from the heat and allow to cool slightly.

2. Combine the flour, brown sugar, cinnamon, and salt in a large bowl. Stir in the browned butter until large crumbs form; set aside.

3. For the cake, preheat the oven to 350°F. Butter and flour a 9-inch square baking pan; set aside.

4. Mix the flour, granulated sugar, baking powder, salt, cinnamon, and orange zest in a large bowl. Set aside.

5. Cook and stir the butter in a skillet over medium heat until it foams, begins to turn brown, and smells nutty. Cool slightly.

6. Combine the egg, milk, orange juice, vanilla, and browned butter in a separate bowl. Pour the egg mixture into the dry ingredients and stir just until combined. Spread the batter in the prepared pan. (It will look like a small amount of batter.) Distribute the cranberries over the batter, pressing them into the batter slightly.

7. Sprinkle the crumb topping evenly over the cake, pressing down on it slightly. (This will be a very generous amount of crumbs.) Bake for about 50 minutes or until the crumbs are golden and a cake tester inserted in the center of the cake comes out clean. Transfer to a wire rack and cool completely in the pan.

BEER-CHEESE FONDUE

Dairy industry employee Kathleen Cuddy of Kansas City, Missouri, was given this recipe by her mother-in-law, Bonnie. "Fondue-ing is a Christmas and Valentine's Day tradition in the Cuddy household," Kathleen says. "Dipping and dunking is a fun way to share a meal with loved ones, and nothing is better than the warm, melty goodness of cheese!"

1 (8-ounce) package shredded sharp Cheddar cheese

1 (8-ounce) package shredded Swiss cheese

2 tablespoons all-purpose flour

½ teaspoon salt

¼ teaspoon freshly ground black pepper

¼ teaspoon paprika

1 garlic clove, peeled

1 (12-ounce) bottle lager-style beer*

1 tablespoon coarse-ground spicy brown mustard

Dash hot pepper sauce

Dippers such as cooked cocktail sausages; bread or soft pretzel chunks; apple wedges; broccoli and cauliflower florets; grape or cherry tomatoes; sugar snap peas; or roasted Brussels sprouts

1. Combine the cheeses, flour, salt, pepper, and paprika in a large mixing bowl. Slice the garlic clove in half. Rub the bottom and sides of a fondue pot or medium saucepan with the cut sides of the garlic.

2. Bring the beer to a simmer in the fondue pot over low heat. Gradually add the cheese mixture, ½ cup at a time, stirring continuously until well blended and smooth. Keep at a low simmer; do not allow the fondue to boil rapidly.

3. Stir in the mustard and hot sauce. Keep the pot over a very low flame to serve. Serve with dippers of choice.

*TIP If you like, nonalcoholic beer works just fine.

CHICKEN FINGER NACHOS

When you need serious party food for big appetites—and tortilla chips are just too wimpy—platter up these crispy chicken fingers drizzled with cheese sauce and topped with an assortment of crispy pickles, peppers, and tomatoes.

2	tablespoons butter
2	tablespoons all-purpose flour
½	teaspoon salt
¼	teaspoon freshly ground black pepper
¼	teaspoon garlic powder
1½	cups milk
1½	cups shredded sharp Cheddar cheese
12	prepared breaded chicken fingers
½	cup dill pickle slices
1	to 2 Roma tomatoes, chopped
¼	cup sliced banana peppers
1	tablespoon chopped fresh chives

1. Melt the butter in a large saucepan over medium heat. Whisk in the flour, salt, pepper, and garlic powder. Cook and stir for 2 to 3 minutes, being careful not to brown or burn the flour mixture.

2. Gradually whisk in the milk until smooth and well blended. Cook, stirring frequently, until thickened. Whisk in the cheese until smooth. Keep warm.

3. Bake the chicken fingers according to the package instructions. Arrange them on a large serving platter. Drizzle with the desired amount of cheese sauce. Top with the dill pickles, tomatoes, banana peppers, and chives. Serve immediately.

FOURTH OF JULY FEAST
Chicken Finger Nachos
Cheese-Stuffed Turkey Burgers (page 67)
Beet and Butter Lettuce Salad with Sour
  Cream–Mustard Dressing (page 168)
Cornmeal Rapsberry Linzer Cookies (page 197)

BUFFALO CHICKEN DIP

When the gang gathers to watch the big game, stir together this creamy dip based on one of the most popular appetizers of all time. The slow cooker makes it melty and keeps it warm.

2 cups chopped cooked chicken breast

2 (8-ounce) packages cream cheese, softened

1 cup blue cheese or ranch salad dressing

¾ cup hot wing sauce

1½ cups shredded Cheddar cheese, divided

Celery and/or carrot sticks, crackers, or tortilla chips

1. Combine the chicken, cream cheese, salad dressing, wing sauce, and half the Cheddar cheese in a large mixing bowl. Stir to mix thoroughly. Transfer to a 2-quart slow cooker. Sprinkle the remaining cheese on top. Cover and cook on low for 2½ to 3 hours or on high for 1½ hours or until melted and bubbling. (If using the high-heat setting, turn the heat to low to keep warm while serving.)

2. Serve with celery and carrot sticks, crackers, or tortilla chips for dipping.

TIP If you prefer an oven method for this dip, combine the chicken, cream cheese, dressing, wing sauce, and half the cheese in a 2-quart baking dish; stir to mix thoroughly. Top with the remaining cheese. Cover and bake at 350°F for 25 to 30 minutes or until heated through and bubbling.

FESTIVE HOLIDAY PARTY
Beer-Cheese Fondue (page 225)
Buffalo Chicken Dip
Artichoke and Roasted Red Pepper Yogurt Dip (page 103)
Salmon Tortilla Rolls (page 113)

CHEESE LOVER'S PIZZA SQUARES

A sweep of creamy ricotta over the crust stands in for sauce on this easy pizza topped with mozzarella, pepperoni, tomatoes, and yellow pepper. Cut it into small squares as a casual nibble to serve to a crowd.

1 (13.8-ounce) tube refrigerated pizza dough

1 cup ricotta cheese

2 cups shredded mozzarella cheese

2 ounces diced pepperoni

2 Roma tomatoes, thinly sliced

1 cup chopped yellow bell pepper

1 teaspoon dried oregano, crushed

2 tablespoons chopped fresh parsley

1. Preheat the oven to 400°F. Press the pizza dough into a 15-by-10-inch baking pan.

2. Bake the crust for 12 minutes. Remove from the oven and spread the ricotta cheese on the crust. Top with the mozzarella cheese, pepperoni, tomatoes, bell pepper, and oregano.

3. Return to the oven and bake for another 6 minutes or until the cheese is melted. Sprinkle with the parsley. Cut into squares and serve.

SMOKY MAC AND CHEESE

Where there's smoke, there's flavor—at least that's what barbecue aficionados say. Smoked Gouda gives this company-worthy mac and cheese a very special touch.

Softened butter, for the baking dish

5 tablespoons butter, divided

¼ cup all-purpose flour

2 cups whole milk

1 pound smoked Gouda cheese, shredded

½ teaspoon freshly ground black pepper

½ teaspoon kosher salt

3 to 4 dashes hot sauce

1½ cups half-and-half

1 pound mostaccioli, cooked according to the package directions

1 cup crushed crackers or seasoned bread crumbs

1. Preheat the oven to 350°F. Butter a 3-quart casserole dish; set aside.

2. Melt 4 tablespoons of the butter in a medium saucepan over medium heat. Whisk in the flour and cook for 1 minute, whisking constantly. Pour in the milk all at once and whisk until smooth. Continue cooking, whisking frequently, until the mixture thickens, about 3 minutes.

3. Reserve 1 cup of the cheese for the topping. Whisk in the remaining cheese a handful at a time until melted. Stir in the pepper, salt, and hot sauce. Stir in the half-and-half.

4. Add the cooked pasta to the cheese sauce and stir until well combined. Pour into the prepared casserole dish.

5. Melt the remaining 1 tablespoon of butter. Combine the cracker crumbs, the melted butter, and the reserved 1 cup shredded cheese in a medium bowl. Toss to combine. Sprinkle evenly over the top of the casserole.

6. Bake for 35 minutes or until the casserole is bubbling and the topping is golden brown. Let the casserole stand for 5 minutes before serving.

Seafood Casserole, page 234

SEAFOOD CASSEROLE

This wild rice–blend casserole studded with shrimp, crab, and vegetables emerges from the oven in a bubbling Parmesan cream sauce. Buttered bread crumbs are a crowning touch. (Recipe pictured on page 232.)

Softened butter, for the baking dish

1½ teaspoons salt, divided

2 (4-ounce) packages long grain and wild rice blend

1 pound small uncooked shrimp, peeled and deveined, tails removed

2 (6-ounce) cans fancy white crabmeat, drained

7 tablespoons butter, divided

1½ cups sliced fresh mushrooms (4 ounces)

2 stalks celery, chopped

1 large shallot, minced

6 tablespoons all-purpose flour

3 cups whole milk

½ cup dry white wine

¼ teaspoon freshly ground black pepper

¼ teaspoon paprika

⅛ teaspoon cayenne

1 cup shredded Parmesan cheese

2 slices soft white bread

2 tablespoons grated Parmesan cheese

¼ cup finely chopped fresh parsley

1. Butter a 9 by 13-inch baking dish; set aside.

2. Preheat the oven to 375°F. Bring 4 cups water and ½ teaspoon of the salt to a boil in a medium saucepan over medium-high heat. Add the rice and stir to mix well. Turn the heat to low. Cover and cook for 40 minutes. Remove the lid and fluff the rice with a fork. (If any water remains in the pan, drain the rice in a fine-mesh strainer.) Transfer the rice to an extra-large bowl; set aside.

3. Bring 4 cups water and a ½ teaspoon of the salt to a boil in a large saucepan. Add the shrimp. When the water returns to a boil, cook the shrimp for 1 minute. Drain immediately. Add the shrimp and drained crabmeat to the rice; set aside.

4. Melt 6 tablespoons of the butter in a large saucepan over medium heat. Add the mushrooms, celery, and shallot; cook, stirring occasionally, until the vegetables are crisp-tender, 3 minutes.

5. Add the flour and cook, stirring constantly, for 1 minute. Slowly add the milk, whisking constantly, until smooth. Cook and stir over medium-low heat until the sauce is thickened, 5 to 6 minutes. Add the wine, black pepper, paprika, and cayenne. Whisk in the shredded Parmesan.

6. Pour the mushroom-wine sauce over the rice and seafood and gently stir to combine. Transfer the mixture to the prepared baking dish.

7. Place the bread slices in a food processor or blender and process into medium-fine crumbs. (You should have about 1 cup soft bread crumbs.) Melt the remaining 1 tablespoon of butter. Toss the bread crumbs with the grated Parmesan and the melted butter. Sprinkle over the casserole. Bake, uncovered, for 35 to 40 minutes or until bubbling and the bread crumbs are golden brown.

8. Let stand for 10 minutes. Sprinkle with the fresh parsley and serve.

CHUNKY BAKED POTATO CHOWDER

All the flavors of a loaded baked potato are stirred into this yummy soup from Lance and Jonna Schutte of Jo-Lane Dairy in Monona, Iowa. The Schuttes are so dedicated to dairy farming that already their three young children—all under the age of six—each have their own registered dairy cow.

4	slices bacon
1	cup chopped onion
½	cup chopped carrot
½	cup chopped celery
6	cups milk
¼	cup all-purpose flour
1	teaspoon paprika
¼	teaspoon salt
¼	teaspoon freshly ground black pepper
1½	cups shredded Cheddar cheese
3	medium unpeeled russet potatoes, baked, cooled, and cut into bite-size pieces
	Hot pepper sauce
2	green onions, sliced

1. Cook the bacon until crisp in a large skillet. Remove the bacon from the skillet, reserving the drippings. Crumble the bacon and set aside.

2. Add the onion, carrot, and celery to the bacon drippings in the skillet and cook over medium heat until tender; set aside.

3. Whisk together the milk, flour, paprika, salt, and pepper in a large saucepan. Bring to a boil and stir for 1 minute or until slightly thickened. Reduce the heat and slowly add the cheese, stirring constantly until melted.

4. Add the cooked onion mixture and potatoes to the soup in the saucepan. Stir well. Heat until all the vegetables are warm. Season to taste with hot pepper sauce. Serve topped with a sprinkling of bacon crumbles and green onion.

TIP You can use reduced-fat milk or fat-free milk, but the chowder won't be quite as rich and creamy as with whole milk. If you'd like the soup thicker, purée 1 cup of the chowder in a blender, then pour it back into the pot. Stir and heat through before serving.

SUPER CHEESY BACON AND ONION POTATO GRATIN

This dish from blogger Carrie Mess (aka "Dairy Carrie") is extremely versatile. Carrie, who works with her husband and his parents on their hundred-head dairy farm in southern Wisconsin, sometimes changes up the cheeses she uses, or uses chicken, ham, or mushrooms in place of the bacon. She loves to make it for family gatherings. "Our farm is about an hour from where my family lives," Carrie says. "I can put this dish in a thermal bag, in the car right out of the oven and in an hour when I get to my grandma's it's perfectly set and ready to be devoured!"

Softened butter, for the baking dish

3 pounds russet potatoes, peeled and very thinly sliced

2 large yellow onions, thinly sliced

3 garlic cloves, minced

3 tablespoons butter

8 ounces bacon, cooked and crumbled

1½ cups shredded smoked Gouda cheese

1 cup shredded Cheddar cheese

1 cup heavy cream

1 cup milk

2 tablespoons all-purpose flour

1 teaspoon salt

½ teaspoon freshly ground black pepper

1 teaspoon Worcestershire sauce

1. Preheat the oven to 350°F. Butter a 9 by 13-inch baking dish with softened butter. Cover the bottom of the baking dish with one-third of the potatoes. Top with one-third of the onions and the garlic. Dot with 1 tablespoon of the butter and sprinkle with one-third of the crumbled bacon. Top with one-third each of the Gouda and Cheddar cheeses. Repeat with the remaining ingredients in two more layers, ending with a layer of cheese on top.

2. Whisk the cream, milk, and flour in a small bowl. Add salt and pepper and stir in the Worcestershire sauce. Pour the cream mixture over the potatoes.

3. Cover the dish with aluminum foil and bake for 1 hour 10 minutes. Remove the foil and return the dish to the oven. Continue to bake for another 20 to 25 minutes or until the potatoes are tender when pierced with a fork and the top is browned and bubbling. Let stand for 10 minutes before serving.

CHEESY GREEN BEAN CASSEROLE

Try a different take on a classic holiday side dish. This version calls for sour cream and cheese in place of canned soup—and swaps in crunchy toasted almonds for crispy onions.

Softened butter, for the baking dish

2 tablespoons butter

1 small onion, halved and thinly sliced

2 cups sliced fresh mushrooms

2 tablespoons all-purpose flour

½ teaspoon salt

¼ teaspoon freshly ground black pepper

½ cup sour cream

1 cup shredded Muenster or mozzarella cheese, divided

1 (16-ounce) package frozen French-style green beans

¼ cup slivered almonds

1. Butter a 1½-quart baking dish with softened butter; set aside. Preheat the oven to 375°F.

2. For the sauce, melt the butter in a large saucepan over medium heat. Cook the onion and mushrooms in the hot butter until the onions are softened, about 6 minutes. Stir in the flour, salt, and pepper; cook, stirring constantly, for 1 minute. Gradually stir in the sour cream. Stir in ½ cup of the shredded cheese; set aside.

3. Cook the green beans with 3 tablespoons water in the microwave on high for 4 minutes, until bright green and still slightly crisp. Drain then fold into the sauce.

4. Transfer the green bean mixture to the prepared baking dish. Sprinkle with the remaining cheese. Bake for 15 minutes. Sprinkle with the almonds. Return to the oven and bake for another 10 to 15 minutes or until the casserole is bubbling and the almonds are golden brown. Let stand for 5 minutes before serving.

MILKING SHORTHORN

THE DUAL-PURPOSE BREED Milking Shorthorns are distant cousins of Beef Shorthorns (cattle in beef herds). The separation between the two lines came in 1900. The red, white, and roan patterns make the Shorthorn a very attractive animal.

STRENGTHS Milking Shorthorn cows are known to be hardy grazers that can survive in a variety of conditions. They average about 1,750 gallons of milk a year.

ORIGIN Northeastern England, in the 1600s. They were among the first cattle breeds to arrive in colonial America.

"WOW" COW Mysha Lady Di was named World Dairy Expo Grand Champion of her breed in 2005.

She was noted for outstanding milk production. One year, she produced more than 3,700 gallons of milk—more than double the breed's average.

"Other breeders of dairy cows knew about Lady Di and would ask about her," says her owner, Marcia Shaver-Floyd of the Mysha Herd in St. Anthony, Iowa. Lady Di is now gone, but she has many offspring extending her legacy.

"She had the show-ring look and type, and the production to back it up," says Marcia. "They don't always go hand in hand. When she went into a show ring, she knew she was supposed to look good, and she did."

PINK ARCTIC FREEZE

Sarah VanOrden of Ovid, New York, is a ninth-generation dairy farmer who produces a soft, creamy artisan cheese called "Morning Glory" from her herd of sixty Brown Swiss cows. (The cheese is named for one of the original cows in the herd.) This refreshing, pretty-in-pink side dish has been a tradition at her family's holiday meals for at least three generations. Her grandmother first shared it in her newspaper column in the 1960s. Although Sarah uses her own cheese in the recipe, cream cheese works just fine.

1   (8-ounce) package cream cheese, softened
2   tablespoons mayonnaise
2   tablespoons sugar
1   (16-ounce) can whole berry cranberry sauce
1   cup crushed pineapple, drained
½   cup chopped walnuts
1   cup heavy cream

1. Combine the cream cheese, mayonnaise, and sugar in a medium mixing bowl and beat with an electric mixer on medium speed until smooth. Stir in the cranberry sauce, pineapple, and walnuts.

2. Whip the heavy cream in a separate chilled medium-size mixing bowl with an electric mixer on medium speed until soft peaks form, 4 to 5 minutes. Fold the whipped cream into the cream cheese mixture.

3. Transfer the cream mixture to a 9-inch square baking dish. Cover with plastic wrap and freeze until firm, at least 4 hours or overnight. Cut into squares to serve.

DAIRYMAN'S THANKSGIVING
Creamy Vegetable Barley Soup (page 61)
Roast turkey with dressing and gravy
Hot Cheesy Potatoes (page 170)
Roasted Brussels sprouts with garlic and olive oil
Pink Arctic Freeze
Pumpkin Date Stack Cake with Mascarpone
  Frosting (page 249)

SPICY WALNUT BUTTERBALLS

Infused with ginger, cinnamon, cloves, nutmeg, and black pepper, these tender cookies get a double coating of powdered sugar for a sweet and spicy treat.

½ cup (1 stick) unsalted butter, softened

½ cup powdered sugar, plus additional for coating, sifted

1 teaspoon vanilla extract

2 cups all-purpose flour

1 teaspoon ground ginger

1 teaspoon ground cinnamon

1 teaspoon ground nutmeg

½ teaspoon ground cloves

½ teaspoon freshly ground black pepper

¼ teaspoon salt

1 cup finely chopped walnuts, toasted

1. Beat the butter and powdered sugar in a large mixing bowl with an electric mixer until light and fluffy. Add the vanilla extract. Beat until combined.

2. Sift the flour, ginger, cinnamon, nutmeg, cloves, pepper, and salt together. Gradually add the dry ingredients to the butter and sugar mixture, beating and scraping down the sides of the bowl once or twice as necessary. Add the walnuts and mix on low speed just until combined. Cover and chill the dough until it is firm but still pliable, about 1 hour.

3. Preheat the oven to 350°F. Scoop out walnut-size pieces of the dough. Roll them into balls and place on a large nonstick baking sheet.

4. Bake for 15 to 18 minutes or until the bottoms of the cookies are lightly golden. (The tops will be set but still fairly pale.)

5. Immediately coat each warm cookie with sifted powdered sugar. Transfer the coated cookies to a wire rack to cool completely. Right before serving, reroll the cookies in additional sifted powdered sugar.

"The kids always have chores to do . . . (We) plan our whole day around what each of us is doing on the farm."—Julie Lourenzo, Oregon dairy farmer

SHANNON & JULIE LOURENZO TILLAMOOK, OREGON

On more than ninety percent of the dairy farms you visit, the cows are black and white—Holsteins. But that's not true on this farm. Shannon and Julie Lourenzo have beautiful grayish-brown cows at Silver Stream Jerseys in Tillamook, Oregon. Shannon grew up with Jerseys and he's always liked them, simple as that. They milk 450 of them now.

"They're very easy to take care of," he says. "They're also very good on feed conversion into milk. While other dairy cows might weigh 1,400 or 1,500 pounds, our mature cows weigh about 1,000 pounds. So they don't eat as much."

There are good reasons for the Lourenzos to like their Jersey cows. The milk from Jersey cows is generally higher in butterfat and protein, which can be made into cheese. The Lourenzos sell their milk to their local creamery, Tillamook, which distributes cheese and dairy products nationally.

The Lourenzos have three children who help on the farm: Brock, nineteen; Lexi, eighteen; and Laci, twelve. "We love the time we get to spend with family working together on the farm," says Julie. "The kids always have chores to do. They may not like them, but they do them anyway," she laughs. "Shannon and I plan our whole day around what each of us is doing on the farm."

Like all good dairy farmers, Shannon says, "We're committed to producing good, wholesome food products, and are very proud of the way we do it."

BALSAMIC STRAWBERRIES WITH RICOTTA CREAM

For Norma Hein, being a dairy farmer has some very personal benefits. She and her husband, Jay, and their three teenage children operate a dairy farm in Celina, Ohio. "I'm a family person," she says. "I get to be around my husband and children. We're down in our milking parlor and the kids are in and out helping, and you get to talk with them. We're always communicating." For this family-favorite dessert, balsamic vinegar complements the sweetness of fruit—particularly strawberries and stone fruits such as peaches, nectarines, and plums in Norma's recipe.

- 2   cups whole-milk ricotta cheese
- 1   (8-ounce) package cream cheese, softened
- ¼   cup powdered sugar
- 1   teaspoon vanilla extract
- 3   tablespoons balsamic vinegar
- 2   tablespoons granulated sugar
- 2   cups fresh strawberries, hulled and quartered
- 1   tablespoon sliced fresh basil leaves

1. Combine the ricotta cheese, cream cheese, powdered sugar, and vanilla extract in a large mixing bowl. Beat with an electric mixer on medium speed until thoroughly blended.

2. Divide the cheese mixture among four 10-ounce glasses or goblets. Cover and refrigerate at least 1 hour or until ready to serve.

3. Combine the vinegar and granulated sugar in a small saucepan and bring to a boil over medium-high heat. Reduce the heat and simmer for 2 or 3 minutes or until the mixture becomes lightly syrupy and easily coats the back of a spoon. Remove from the heat and allow to cool completely.

4. Toss the strawberries with the balsamic syrup until coated. Divide the strawberries evenly among the glasses over the chilled cheese mixture. Top with ribbons of basil and serve immediately.

PUMPKIN DATE STACK CAKE WITH MASCARPONE FROSTING

Mascarpone is an Italian-style double cream cheese. Combined with cream cheese, butter, powdered sugar, and vanilla, it is a lovely frosting for this moist autumnal cake.

CAKE
- ¾ cup (1½ sticks) unsalted butter, plus more for the pans
- 2 cups cake flour, plus more for the pans
- 1 teaspoon baking soda
- 2 teaspoons baking powder
- 1 teaspoon ground cinnamon
- ½ teaspoon ground nutmeg
- ¼ teaspoon ground cloves
- ¼ teaspoon salt
- 1½ cups granulated sugar
- 3 tablespoons molasses
- 3 large eggs
- 1 cup pumpkin purée
- ½ cup buttermilk
- 2 teaspoons vanilla extract
- 1 cup pitted chopped dates

FROSTING
- 4 ounces cream cheese, softened
- 4 tablespoons butter, softened
- 2½ cups powdered sugar, sifted
- 1 teaspoon vanilla extract
- 8 ounces mascarpone cheese, at room temperature
- Chopped pitted dates, for garnish

1. For the cake, preheat the oven to 350°F. Butter and flour three 8-inch round cake pans; set aside.

2. Sift the cake flour, baking soda, baking powder, cinnamon, nutmeg, cloves, and salt into a medium bowl; set aside.

3. Beat the butter and granulated sugar in a large mixing bowl with an electric mixer on medium speed until light and fluffy, 3 minutes. Add the molasses and blend thoroughly. Add the eggs one at a time, beating well after each addition.

4. Whisk together the pumpkin, buttermilk, and vanilla extract in a separate bowl. Alternately add the dry ingredients and pumpkin mixture to the butter mixture in three additions, beating on low speed after each addition until combined. Stir in the dates.

5. Divide the batter among the prepared pans. Bake for 30 minutes or until a cake tester inserted in the cake layers comes out clean. Transfer to wire racks; cool for 10 minutes. Remove the cakes from the pans and cool completely on the racks.

6. For the frosting, beat the cream cheese and butter in a small mixing bowl with the mixer on medium speed just until smooth and creamy. Gradually beat in the powdered sugar. Add the vanilla extract. Add the mascarpone cheese and beat until smooth.

7. To assemble the cake, place one cake layer on a serving plate. Spread with one-third of the frosting. Top with the second layer and spread with one-third of the frosting. Top with the third layer and spread with the remaining frosting. Chill for at least 1 hour. Sprinkle the cake with additional chopped dates before serving.

METRIC CONVERSIONS AND EQUIVALENTS

METRIC CONVERSION FORMULAS

To Convert	Multiply
Ounces to grams	Ounces by 28.35
Pounds to kilograms	Pounds by.454
Teaspoons to milliliters	Teaspoons by 4.93
Tablespoons to milliliters	Tablespoons by 14.79
Fluid ounces to milliliters	Fluid ounces by 29.57
Cups to milliliters	Cups by 236.59
Cups to liters	Cups by .236
Pints to liters	Pints by .473
Quarts to liters	Quarts by .946
Gallons to liters	Gallons by 3.785
Inches to centimeters	Inches by 2.54

APPROXIMATE METRIC EQUIVALENTS

Volume

¼ teaspoon	1 milliliter
½ teaspoon	2.5 milliliters
¾ teaspoon	4 milliliters
1 teaspoon	5 milliliters
1¼ teaspoon	6 milliliters
1½ teaspoon	7.5 milliliters
1¾ teaspoon	8.5 milliliters
2 teaspoons	10 milliliters
1 tablespoon (½ fluid ounce)	15 milliliters
2 tablespoons (1 fluid ounce)	30 milliliters
¼ cup	60 milliliters
⅓ cup	80 milliliters
½ cup (4 fluid ounces)	120 milliliters
⅔ cup	160 milliliters
¾ cup	180 milliliters
1 cup (8 fluid ounces)	240 milliliters
1¼ cups	300 milliliters
1½ cups (12 fluid ounces)	360 milliliters
1⅔ cups	400 milliliters
2 cups (1 pint)	460 milliliters
3 cups	700 milliliters
4 cups (1 quart)	0.95 liter
1 quart plus ¼ cup	1 liter
4 quarts (1 gallon)	3.8 liters

Weight

¼ ounce	7 grams
½ ounce	14 grams
¾ ounce	21 grams
1 ounce	28 grams
1¼ ounces	35 grams
1½ ounces	42.5 grams
1⅔ ounces	45 grams
2 ounces	57 grams
3 ounces	85 grams
4 ounces (¼ pound)	113 grams
5 ounces	142 grams
6 ounces	170 grams
7 ounces	198 grams
8 ounces (½ pound)	227 grams
16 ounces (1 pound)	454 grams
35.25 ounces (2.2 pounds)	1 kilogram

Length

⅛ inch	3 millimeters
¼ inch	6 millimeters
½ inch	1¼ centimeters
1 inch	2½ centimeters
2 inches	5 centimeters
2½ inches	6 centimeters
4 inches	10 centimeters
5 inches	13 centimeters
6 inches	15¼ centimeters
12 inches (1 foot)	30 centimeters

OVEN TEMPERATURES

To convert Fahrenheit to Celsius, subtract 32 from Fahrenheit, multiply the result by 5, then divide by 9.

Description	Fahrenheit	Celsius	British Gas Mark
Very cool	200°	95°	0
Very cool	225°	110°	¼
Very cool	250°	120°	½
Cool	275°	135°	1
Cool	300°	150°	2
Warm	325°	165°	3
Moderate	350°	175°	4
Moderately hot	375°	190°	5
Fairly hot	400°	200°	6
Hot	425°	220°	7
Very hot	450°	230°	8
Very hot	475°	245°	9

COMMON INGREDIENTS AND THEIR APPROXIMATE EQUIVALENTS

1 cup uncooked white rice = 185 grams
1 cup all-purpose flour = 140 grams
1 stick butter (4 ounces · ½ cup · 8 tablespoons) = 110 grams
1 cup butter (8 ounces · 2 sticks · 16 tablespoons) = 220 grams
1 cup brown sugar, firmly packed = 225 grams
1 cup granulated sugar = 200 grams

Information compiled from a variety of sources, including *Recipes into Type* by Joan Whitman and Dolores Simon (Newton, MA: Biscuit Books, 2000); *The New Food Lover's Companion* by Sharon Tyler Herbst (Hauppauge, NY: Barron's, 1995); and *Rosemary Brown's Big Kitchen Instruction Book* (Kansas City, MO: Andrews McMeel, 1998).

INDEX

Andrews McMeel Publishing, LLC
an Andrews McMeel Universal Company
1130 Walnut Street, Kansas City, Missouri 64106

www.andrewsmcmeel.com

15 16 17 18 19 SHO 10 9 8 7 6 5 4 3 2

ISBN 978-1-4494-6503-2

Library of Congress Control Number: 2014955687

Produced by Blue Trellis, LLC
Publisher/Editorial Director: Linda Raglan Cunningham
Executive Editor: Carl Raymond

Editorial Development: Waterbury Publications, Inc.
Book Design & Art Direction: Ken Carlson
Food photography: Peter Krumhart and Dean Tanner
Photography by Hoard's Dairyman: 13, 62, 63, 110, 111, 150, 151,
     166, 184, 185, and 241
Photography by Lisa Perrin Dubravec: 14, 39, 63, 109, 111, 150,
     151, 166, 184, 210, 216-217, 240, and 241

Andrews McMeel Publishing, LLC
Editor: Jean Z. Lucas
Art Director: Tim Lynch
Production Editor: Maureen Sullivan
Production Manager: Carol Coe
Demand Planner: Sue Eikos

ATTENTION: SCHOOLS AND BUSINESSES
Andrews McMeel books are available at quantity discounts with bulk
purchase for educational, business, or sales promotional use. For
information, please e-mail the Andrews McMeel Publishing Special
Sales Department: specialsales@amuniversal.com.